QUICK-STRIP PAPER PIECING

FOR BLOCKS, BORDERS & QUILTS

PEGGY MARTIN

C&T PUBLISHING INC.

Text © 2003, Phyllis Golloway Marlin
Artwork © 2003, C&T Publishing
Editor-in-Chief: Darra Williamson
Editor: Pamela Mostek
Technical Editors: Carolyn Aune, Joan Hyme
Copyeditor/Proofreader: Linda Dease Smith, Carol Barrett
Cover Designer: Kristen Yenche
Book Designer: Staci Harpole, Cubic Design
Design Director: Diane Pedersen
Illustrator: Mary Ann Tenorio
Production Assistant: Tim Manibusan
Digital Photography: Diane Pedersen and Luke Mulks
Published by C&T Publishing, Inc., P.O. Box 1456, Lafayette, California, 94549

Front cover: *Rainbow Galaxy*
Back cover: *The Dawning*

Library of Congress Cataloging-in-Publication Data
Martin, Peggy.
 Quick-strip paper piecing : for blocks, borders & quilts / Peggy Martin.
  p. cm.
Includes bibliographical references and index.
 ISBN 1-57120-216-1 (paper trade)
 1. Patchwork--Patterns. 2. Quilting. 3. Patchwork quilts. I. Title.

TT835.M273614 2003
746.46--dc21

                2003011827

Printed in China
10 9 8 7 6 5 4 3 2 1

Dedication

I dedicate this book to all my students over the years whose enthusiasm and support brought sunshine into my life and who continue to excite and inspire me to make more and better quilts. I also dedicate it to my family, my husband David and sons Michael and Ryan, who put up with the mounds of fabric all over the house, the fast-food meals when I have deadlines, and who continue to give me reasons to get out there and teach!

Acknowledgments

I would like to give a big thank you to all the quilters who contributed their time and talents to design and make quilts for the book—Nancy Amidon, Jeanne Backman, Kris Blundell-Mitchell, Lorraine Marstall, Sandra McCullough, Jean Nagy, Allegra Olson, Lois Russell, Karen Shell, Mary Tabar, Wanzie Walley, and Patricia Wolfe.

Thanks to Amidon Quiltworks for providing a workshop space.

My special appreciation goes to the talented long-arm machine quilters—Laurie Daniells, Wendy Knight, Carolyn Reynolds, and Lisa Taylor whose artistic quilting added so much to my quilts.

And a special thank you to the staff of C&T, especially editors Pamela Mostek and Carolyn Aune, who helped me through the labyrinth of writing a first book.

Table of Contents

what's
inside

Introduction

When I took my first quilting class over twenty years ago, each piece was marked and cut out one at a time with a template, and each block was hand pieced. It took me an entire evening to cut out one block and several evenings to hand piece it. It was definitely a slow process.

Later, I took another sewing class, but this time we cut out multiple units at once (still using scissors and templates) and chain pieced them at the sewing machine, marking the machine with a quarter-inch seam allowance instead of marking on each fabric piece. About this time a light bulb went on in my head – maybe there were quicker, easier ways to get the same accurate result!

Soon after that we began using the rotary cutter and discovered methods to cut out triangles and squares and even more time was saved. From that time on I was a convert— always looking for faster, easier ways to do accurate piecing. When I began teaching over 18 years ago, I always tried to streamline methods that I learned from books and patterns in order to make them more time-saving, efficient, and fun.

Throughout my quilting career I've continued to search for the quickest, most accurate way to create beautiful quilts. I began experimenting with paper piecing in recent years because it makes it possible to piece very complex blocks almost effortlessly. However, foundation piecing is often a slow process and can be quite time-consuming. With my usual determination to find the most time-saving and efficient techniques, I began developing an even faster way to paper piece complex blocks.

The result of that experimenting is my first book, *Quick-Strip Paper Piecing*, which will show you how to apply the principles of strip piecing in an assembly-line fashion to make the repeat units used in paper-pieced blocks.

Using this method, you will be able to piece blocks with repeat units in a fraction of the time, and because strip measurements are given for each area of the block, you will make fewer mistakes and waste less fabric.

I began developing the designs and patterns for this technique so that I could teach them to my students. I was pleased to discover that experienced paper piecers were amazed at how much faster blocks could be pieced, and quilters new to paper piecing found it a very easy way to begin.

In the Quick-Strip Paper-Piecing section, you will find step-by-step instructions for the technique. Read through the directions, look at the easy-to-follow photos, and you will be ready to begin. Refer back to this section as you create the blocks and quilts if you need more information.

In the Gallery of Quilts, I've included an outstanding collection of quilts, many of which were made by my students. I hope they will help inspire you to make your own beautiful quilt while exploring the possibilities of *Quick-Strip Paper Piecing*.

Peggy

Preparing to Sew

The first step in making a quilt is just getting ready. Clearing off your workspace, cleaning and oiling your sewing machine, and assembling all the tools and supplies needed for the project will help get you going.

sewing

Preparing to Sew

Before you begin your Quick-Strip Paper-Piecing project, make sure that you have all the supplies assembled. Here I've included a list of what you will need. Many of them you probably use for other quilting projects, and a few others may be new to you but are very helpful for this technique.

Tools and Supplies

Sewing machine with sewing extension surface or cabinet

Open-toe foot (optional) — This enables you to see the sewing line more easily.

Sewing machine needles — Use size 90/14 or size 80/12 quilting, jeans/denim, or universal needles for paper piecing. Use size 70/10 or 75/11 quilting, jeans/denim, or universal needles for appliqué of curved seams.

Neutral sewing thread for piecing — Use thread that will blend best with your project.

Rotary cutter, mat, and ruler for cutting strips and for trimming up blocks and projects

Spray starch — This will minimize stretching and distortion of the fabric as the edges of paper-pieced blocks are often off-grain. You can apply the spray starch after your strips are cut if you don't want to starch a large piece of fabric. Just spray each strip and iron.

Invisible tape — Use it to reinforce a sewing line on a paper pattern when it becomes torn after ripping out stitching or to join paper sections for borders.

Glue stick — This is for basting appliqué of curved seams in the New York Beauty project.

Fabric scissors

Paper scissors

Seam ripper

Selecting Your Fabrics

Each pattern has a lined sketch of the block and a color photo to help you get started on your own quilt plan. Notice that the sewn block and the lined drawings are the reverse of the pattern, which is what happens in paper piecing. You can photocopy the lined drawings and try out different color combinations with colored pencils or fabric mock-ups.

Selecting the background fabric first often makes other fabric choices easier because the value (lightness or darkness) of the background fabric will affect the values of the other fabrics chosen. For example, if you choose a dark background, choose light or light-medium fabrics for star points or other design elements if you want to create a strong contrast. If the background is light, then design elements from darker fabrics will be more dramatic. Just be sure to have a good contrast with the background fabric for best definition of star points.

Some block patterns have suggested areas for background fabric indicated in the project. Changing the background and colored areas of a block pattern can greatly alter the look of a block. Look at the effect that changing a background area has on the Spinning Star blocks below:

Spinning Star block by Peggy Martin

Spinning Star block by Wanzie Walley

Types of Print Fabric

Fabrics which read as "solid" such as tone-on-tone prints, batiks, hand-dyed fabrics, or mottled solids, work well just about anywhere in these blocks and are perfect for small areas such as star points. You can use smaller-scale prints as well in many areas. Large-scale prints generally work best in larger areas of a design but can be unpredictable or even exciting when used in other areas.

Directional fabrics or small stripes can be more challenging to use but can produce some interesting effects. In *Rainbow Galaxy*, page 52, I used several different small-scale stripes in the blocks, adding movement and excitement.

Fiber Content

Cotton is my fabric of choice for most quilting projects because of its ease in sewing, pressing, and laundering. Prewash cotton fabrics, then press with spray starch to help prevent stretching when blocks are off-grain, which often occurs in paper piecing. Because fabrics are sewn to a paper foundation, other types of fabric such as silks or metallics can be sewn with relative ease; however, take special care in pressing and laundering when using these fabrics. Many will melt under a hot iron, so I advise using a lower heat setting.

Also protect the fabric with a press cloth if it tends to stick to the iron. If any of your fabrics can't be washed, washing of the completed projects will not be possible. The quilt will need to be dry cleaned if necessary. For this reason, use non-cotton fabrics on wall quilts, which do not need frequent laundering.

Making the Patterns

Now that you have your fabric and supplies assembled, you're ready to make the copies of the paper patterns you will need for each project. Each block in this book is made up of several identical pattern units that are repeated. You will need a paper pattern for each repeat unit. Each block tells you how many copies you will need in order to make the block. I suggest several ways to copy the patterns as you will see below. Choose the option that you prefer.

Copy Machine

This is my favorite method because it's fast and simple to make photocopies of the pattern. Make one test copy first, then hold it up to the light with the original to see if it is an exact copy. If it varies even slightly, don't use it. Try another copier, or see if the copier can be adjusted to make the copies accurate. This is extremely important. If the paper copy is not true, you won't be able to sew the blocks together precisely.

Many people have copier/printers or scanners on their home computers, which often work well for paper-piecing copies.

I generally use regular 20-weight copy paper, which is somewhat thick, but keeps its shape well when piecing. Using your home copier or scanner enables you to experiment with other types of paper, such as vellum, tracing paper, or newsprint. Again, always check for accuracy when making copies. Another advantage in using a copier is that patterns can be enlarged or reduced to make different size blocks. For example, to enlarge a 12" block to a 15" block, copy the pattern at 125%. See page 24 for a chart with percentages to use for making the blocks a different size.

Sewing Machine Copies

You can make multiple copies at one time using your sewing machine by perforating layers of paper with your needle. Trace or photocopy one accurate copy of the pattern and staple it to several layers of typing paper, freezer paper, or foundation-piecing paper. Staple only in the background areas, not over any of the lines of the pattern.

Take the thread from the top of your machine and remove the bobbin. Using a size 80/12 or 90/14 needle and a short stitch length (16–18 stitches per inch or 1.5–2.0 per centimeter) sew exactly along all the lines of the pattern, including the outside lines.

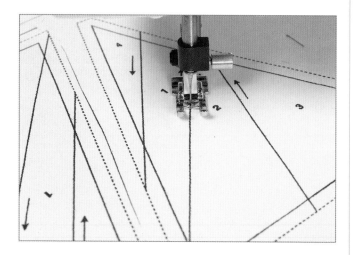

Hold the pattern up to the light to make sure you haven't missed any lines. Remove the staples. Transfer all markings to each pattern in the appropriate spaces using a permanent pen.

Cutting Out the Patterns

After you have made copies of the patterns, cut them out on the outer line using paper scissors or an old rotary cutting blade. The patterns in the book include the ¼" seam allowance on the pattern. Most beginners will find it easier when the seam allowance is included; however, some advanced piecers opt to cut off the seam allowance on the paper because bulk is reduced when joining units. If you decide to leave the seam allowance off the paper, remember to add it to the fabric when you are trimming the block.

Cutting Strips for Foundation Piecing

Once you have decided on a color scheme for your block, selected your fabrics, and made copies of your patterns, you are ready to cut strips. Each strip is cut from selvage to selvage and is approximately 40" long. The width of strip needed for each area of a pattern is indicated on the pattern as well as in the cutting instructions for each project.

Strips do not need to be cut precisely; the size shown on the pattern is the minimum size strip that will work easily. Strips can always be wider than needed if you have extra strips remaining from another project that you want to use. Just be sure that the strip is at least as wide as indicated on the pattern.

Getting Started

◆ To prepare your sewing machine for paper piecing, insert a new size 80/12 or 90/14 quilting, jeans/denim, or universal needle.

◆ Set the stitch length shorter than normal—about 16–18 stitches per inch or 1.5–2.0 per centimeter, depending on your machine. This makes seams stronger and also helps perforate the paper, making removal easier.

◆ Set your iron on the cotton setting with no steam. Steam can cause your paper to wilt or curl up when ironing. Protect your ironing surface by covering it with a piece of muslin or other light-colored fabric if you are using photocopied foundations. Ironing over photocopy ink can cause ink to transfer to any surface it touches, including your ironing board cover, your iron, or the fabric in your blocks. If your iron accidentally touches the ink, be sure to clean it thoroughly.

Quick-Strip Paper Piecing

This simple, time-saving technique applies strip piecing and assembly-line methods to paper piecing. Beginners find it an easy way to start; more experienced paper piecers find it a real time-saver. But most of all—it's a lot of fun!

technique

Quick-Strip Paper Piecing

Now that you've assembled your fabric and materials, copied your paper patterns, and prepared your sewing machine, you're ready to start this new paper-piecing technique.

In this section, you will find a step-by-step explanation and photos of how to Quick-Strip Paper Piece the Spinning Star block and other patterns and borders. I suggest you read through the directions, looking at the photos as you go. After reading through the steps once, you'll be ready to follow the steps and create your own block. The steps are the same for all the blocks in the book, so you may want to refer back to this section as you make the blocks in the quilt projects.

I designed these patterns to make them easy, fun to use, and as mistake-proof as possible. Each paper foundation pattern has different lines, numbers, and arrows printed on it. Look at the example of the Spinning Star block pattern, which requires eight patterns to make a 12" block. Notice the explanation of the markings printed on the block.

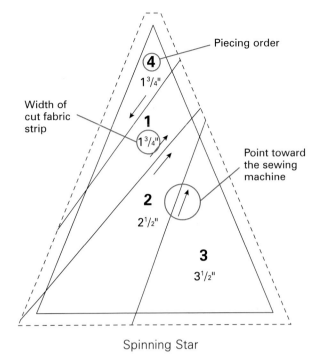

Spinning Star

> *** TIP**
>
> Be sure to allow enough fabric on the strip when laying the units down and when trimming so that you cover the entire area plus a ¼" seam allowance. This is especially important at the points of each pattern piece.

The number of strips you will need to cut for each project is included on the cutting chart.

Notice that the sewing lines extend into the outer ¼" seam allowance. When paper piecing, the stitching should go all the way into the seam allowance. These drawn lines help you begin and end the sewing lines accurately.

The large **bold numbers** indicate the order in which the strips will be sewn, in this example from 1 to 4.

Arrows in each area help position the pattern piece on the fabric strip for the easiest sewing, using the guidelines below.

Numbers with inch marks (") indicate the width of fabric strip to cut for that area. In the Spinning Star the strip size for area 1 is $1^3/_4$".

Guidelines for Sewing the Units

To make Quick-Strip Paper Piecing simple and accurate, here are a few guidelines to keep in mind as you sew. They will help keep mistakes to a minimum... with less ripping out to be done!

1 Always keep the seam allowances to the right. This is the way we normally sew seams, so sewing the foundation seams in the same way is easy to remember. The patterns are designed to be used in this way, and the arrows in the next step are placed to work with the seam allowances on the right.

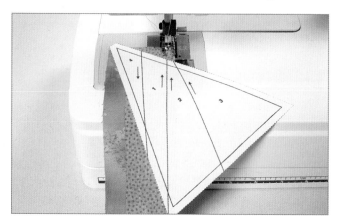

2 Arrows in the new section that you will add point away from you toward the sewing machine. This helps you position the pattern correctly. The new section being added to the paper will always be to the right of the needle when sewing; the previously sewn section with the lower number will be to the left.

Making the Pattern Pieces

The following step-by-step instructions will show you how to make the paper-pieced units for the Spinning Star Block. You will follow these same general steps to make paper-pieced units for other blocks in the book. You may find it helpful to refer back to this section as you construct the other blocks.

1 Make eight copies of the Spinning Star pattern on page 30. Cut out the patterns on the outer seam allowance lines.

2 Refer to the pattern and chart on page 27 for the number and width of the strips needed to complete the block.

3 In the first step of every pattern, both strips 1 and 2 will be added at the same time. Place fabric strip 1 and fabric strip 2 with right sides together and with strip 1 on top. Align them so that the seam allowance is on the right side, just as if you were sewing them together with a standard $\frac{1}{4}$" seam. Lay these strips on your sewing machine throat plate.

4 Look at the paper pattern and find the line between area 1 and area 2. This is the line on which you will be sewing. Position the pattern so that area 1 is to the left and area 2 is to the right. The arrows in both sections should point toward the sewing machine. Look at your fabric strips on the throat plate and visualize where the ¼" seam will fall. Lay the paper pattern on the fabric strips so that the line between area 1 and area 2 falls on the ¼" seam line. Make sure the pattern is positioned down far enough that there is fabric under the top point of area 1 including the seam allowance. Sew across the paper on the drawn line.

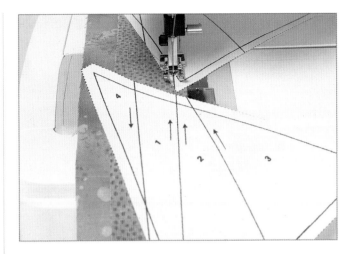

You will find on the Spinning Star pattern, just as on some other patterns in the book, that all 8 units will not fit on one set of strips. Insert the second set of strips, oriented as before, and continue sewing down the remaining units.

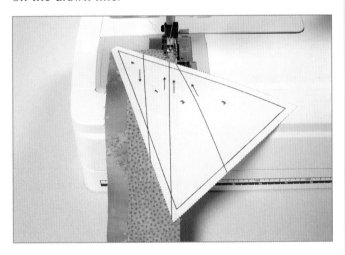

5 Continue down the strip, laying the remaining patterns on the strip in exactly the same way. The patterns can be butted up to each other. Make sure the raw edges of your fabric strips stay aligned on the right side as you sew.

6 Cut the threads and remove the sewn strips from the sewing machine. Open out fabric strip 2 from strip 1, but do not press yet. Flip the strips over so that the papers are on top, making sure strip 2 stays opened. Cut the units apart with scissors. When cutting the units apart, follow the angle of the paper and look at the paper pattern to be sure you do not accidentally trim too close to the areas you are piecing. Make sure there is enough fabric to cover the area plus at least a ¼" seam allowance.

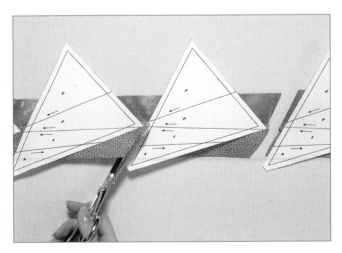

7 Using a dry iron on a protected ironing surface, press all eight units on the fabric side by opening out strip 2 with the iron.

8 Trim away the excess fabric close to the edge of the paper. You don't need to trim precisely yet; that can come later.

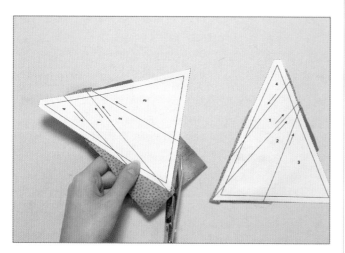

9 Lay strip 3 on your machine throat plate with the right side up. Find the line between area 2 and area 3 and position the paper pattern so the line is ¼" from the right raw edge of the strip. The arrow in area 3 should point toward the machine. Sew across the line. Lay down and sew the other 7 units in the same way. It is all right to overlap the patterns.

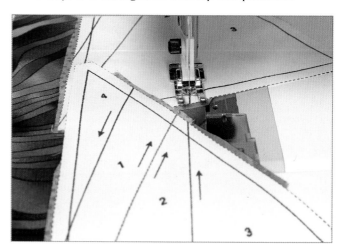

10 Remove the sewn units from the machine. Open out strip 3 and cut the units apart, lifting the foundations as needed to avoid cutting through the paper.

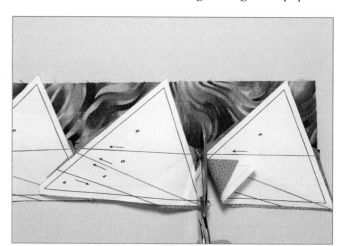

11 For every strip added after numbers 1 and 2, there will be excess fabric in the seams. With the fabric side facing toward you, fold the paper away from behind the seam.

12 Using scissors, trim excess fabric to ¼" seam allowance.

13 Press open strip 3 on all units, and again you may choose to trim away any excess fabric that extends beyond the outer edge of the foundation.

14 Follow the same steps to add strip 4. In order to position the pattern so the arrow points toward the sewing machine, you will need to turn the pattern upside down.

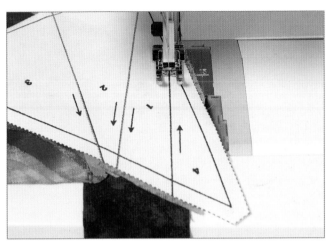

15 Cut the units apart, as before, and trim the excess fabric in the seam allowance as described in steps 11 and 12. Press.

16 When all the fabric strips have been added, use a rotary cutter to precisely trim ¼" from the seam line around all the edges. The pattern pieces can now be sewn into an octagon to make the block.

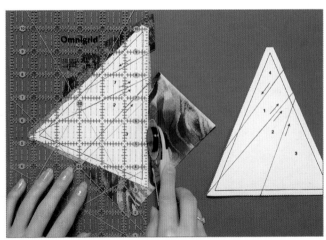

Patterns with Indented Lines

The Spinning Star block just shown is one of the easiest to sew using the Quick-Strip Paper-Piecing method because the pattern units have sewing lines that completely cross the block from edge to edge. Other patterns have indented lines, which are design lines that stop somewhere in the middle of the block. Compare the Spinning Star design with the Twisted Star.

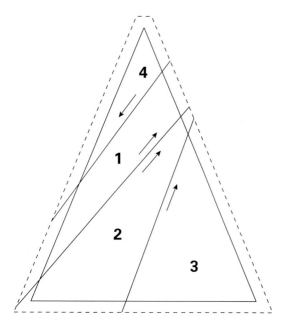

Spinning Star
All sewing lines extend from edge to edge.

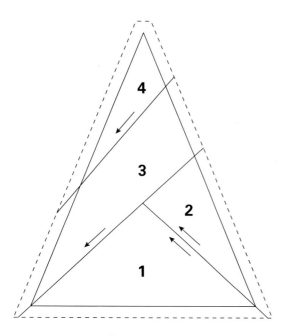

Twisted Star
Sewing line between area 1 and area 2 is indented.

When you sew patterns with indented lines, here are a few important tips to keep in mind:

◆ Begin or end sewing 2 or 3 stitches beyond the drawn line. Depending on how far the line is indented, placement can sometimes be a bit confusing. Place the paper piece where you think the ¼" seam will be, then lift the paper and check for the ¼" seam by "peeking" underneath if you need to be sure you have placed it properly.

◆ If you have trouble placing the sewing line along the ¼" seam line of the strips, try holding up the paper with strips underneath so the light shines through. This should help you find the seam line.

◆ Begin sewing a couple of stitches before the line, and end a couple of stitches past the line. After sewing the first paper unit, place the next paper on the strip. Lift the presser foot and "slide" down to the next indented line. Stitch as before, beginning a couple of stitches before the line. Continue adding units until all are sewn.

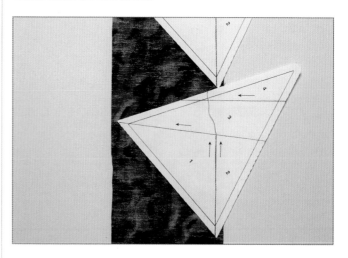

When cutting these units apart, notice how long the point of an area is; be sure to leave enough fabric under this area—especially at the end of a strip. Continue piecing along the strips in order until all areas are completed. Trim the units on the edge of the outer ¼" seam line.

◆ On some patterns, if you feel too much of the strip would be wasted, the paper can be folded down to take up less space on the fabric strip.

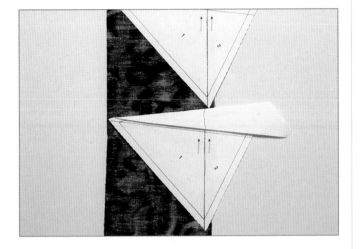

Sewing Together the Block

The following step-by-step instructions will show you how to sew together the paper-pieced units to make the Spinning Star block. You may find it helpful to refer back to this section as you sew together other blocks in the book.

1 Begin by sewing the 8 pattern pieces together into pairs. Carefully remove the paper in the seam allowances to avoid bulk. With the narrow points toward you, press the seams to the left.

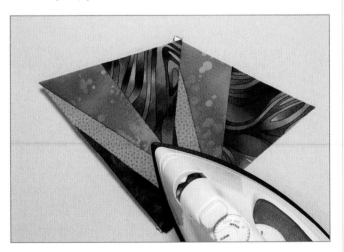

2 Join the pairs into two groups of 4, pressing the seams to the left. Remove the paper in the seam allowances to eliminate bulk.

3 Join the halves to make the octagon.

Remove the paper in the seam allowances before pressing. To reduce bulk in the center of the block so that you can press the seams around in a circle, remove the few stitches from the two previous seams down to the last sewn seam. These are seams that are perpendicular to the last seam.

This will allow you to press all the seams in a circle, "splitting" the last center seam by pressing the right side of the seam down and the left side of the seam up. The very center of the block will open up, greatly reducing bulk in the center.

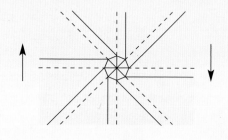

4 For the corner triangles of the block, cut two 4½" squares of background fabric. Cut both squares once diagonally to make four half-square triangles. Sew the triangles to the four corners of the octagon and press toward the triangles. The triangles are slightly oversized so that you can trim the finished block to 12½" square.

Removing the Paper

Leave the paper on as long as you can, ideally until the block is sewn into the quilt. Sometimes I find the blocks become so bulky with paper that they will not press flat, so I remove the paper before that time. If you have spray starched your strips, the paper can be removed carefully before the blocks are completely finished. Sometimes I even remove the paper when the units are finished before I sew them together. Just remember that edges will be off-grain and be careful not to stretch fabric when sewing and pressing.

To remove the paper, fold and crease on the stitching line, then carefully tear it away, "supporting" the seam behind with the finger or thumb of the other hand. Try not to stretch or distort the fabric as you tear the paper. I find it easiest to work on a flat surface, such as a tabletop or lap board to help prevent distortion.

Remove the paper in the reverse order that it was sewn. In other words, remove the paper from the last seam first, then work backwards. If you left the paper in when you joined the block together, remove the paper from the 1/4" seams first, then proceed to remove it from each pattern piece, beginning with the highest number.

Matching Points

◆ In the Spinning Star example, there were no star points or intersections to match. On other blocks, however, you may need to match points when sewing units together. To match points easily, place a positioning pin through the point where the two units need to match.

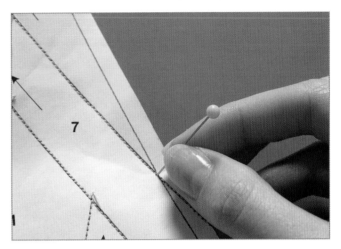

◆ Pin on either side of the positioning pin or, if your paper is too thick to easily pin through, place a paper clip on either side of the pin. With your sewing machine, sew a few large basting stitches in the 1/4" seam in the area where the points need to match, removing the pins or paper clips as you come to them.

◆ Open out the two units and check the matching point on the front. If it is good, go ahead and sew the seam. If it doesn't match exactly, it is easy to remove the few basting stitches and try again.

Correcting Mistakes

No matter how careful we are, sometimes we all make mistakes. When this happens, rip out seams on the fabric side by lifting the fabric strip up and breaking the stitches with a seam ripper. If the paper foundation has been weakened or torn, place a piece of invisible tape over the sewing line. It can easily be sewn through and is easy to tear during paper removal.

Paper Piecing Other Patterns and Borders

As you make blocks or quilts in the book using Quick-Strip Paper Piecing, you will find variations to the technique you've learned in this chapter. Refer back to this section for more information whenever it is helpful or noted in the individual block or quilt instructions.

New York Beauty Pieced Arc

Although the shape of the New York Beauty pattern A differs from the pattern pieces for the stars, the quick-strip piecing method is the same. To begin, with right sides together, lay fabric strip 1 on top of strip 2. Position the paper pattern on top with area 1 to the left and area 2 to the right. The arrows in both sections should point toward the sewing machine. Sew across the paper on the drawn line. Continuing down the strip, position the remaining patterns the same way. Open out fabric strip 2 and cut the units apart as shown on page 16. Add strip 3 and continue paper-piecing in the same manner to complete each New York Beauty pattern A.

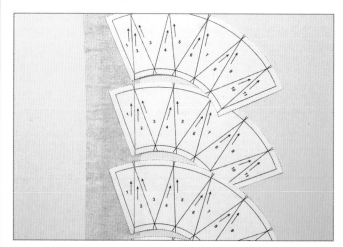

Border with Points

1 The technique for this border is the same. You will piece 4 of the paper border strips at a time on a strip. With right sides together, lay fabric strip 1 on top of strip 2. Position the paper border strip on the fabric strips so that the line between area 1 and area 2 falls on the ¼" seam line with area 1 to the left and area 2 to the right. The arrows in both sections should point toward the sewing machine. Sew across the paper on the drawn line. Continuing down the strip, position 3 more patterns the same way. Open out fabric strip 2 and cut the units apart as shown on page 16. Press.

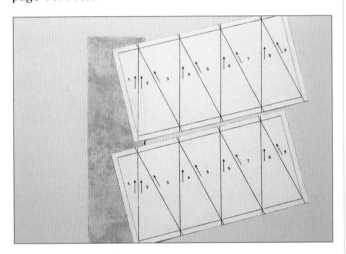

2 Continue paper piecing in the same manner to complete each border up to area 7.

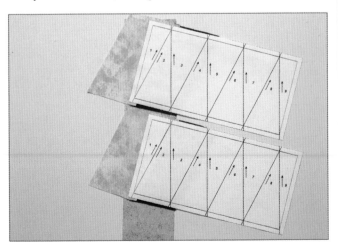

3 After adding area 7, attach another paper border strip. To join the border strips so that there will be a continuous pattern of diamonds with no joining seam, add paper border strips as you make the border. To add a new paper border strip, cut off the seam allowance to the left of area 1 on the new strip. Align the new strip to the pieced strip where indicated and tape in position. Continue paper piecing areas 8 and 9. Area 9 and area 1 of the new paper strips will be combined into a whole background area. Continue paper piecing and adding paper border strips until you have the needed border length.

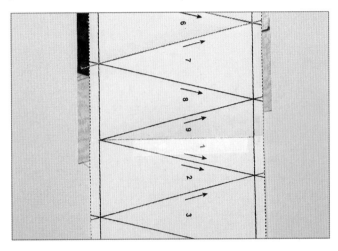

Flying Geese Borders

To paper piece the Flying Geese border, sew groups of geese at the same time on a strip. You can do 4 at a time, 6 at a time, or all 12 at a time, depending on how you want to strip piece them and how many fabrics you want repeated. Fold the paper down when sewing the diagonal lines to avoid wasting too much fabric on each strip.

1 With right sides together, lay fabric strip 1 on top of strip 2. Position the paper border strip on the fabric strips so that the line between area 1 and area 2 falls on the $\frac{1}{4}$" seam line with area 1 to the left and area 2 to the right. The arrows in both sections should point toward the sewing machine. Sew across the paper on the drawn line. Continuing down the strip, position the remaining patterns the same way. Open out fabric strip 2 and cut the units apart as shown on page 16.

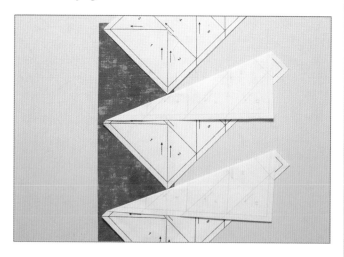

2 Continue paper piecing the border strips until you have completed the needed border length. Note how the paper is folded up to save strip space before placing the next pattern.

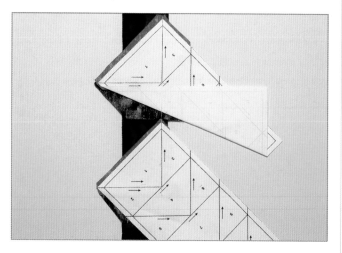

Adapting Other Patterns

Now that you know the process for Quick-Strip Paper Piecing, you may want to make some of the blocks in different sizes. Following is a handy reference chart that includes the percentages to use in order to enlarge or reduce the pattern pieces for a particular block size.

Size of block in the book	Size of block you want to make				
	6" Block	9" Block	12" Block	15" Block	18" Block
6" Block	100%	150%	200%	250%	300%
12" Block	50%	75%	100%	125%	150%

Please note that some of the more complex stars probably should not be reduced a great deal because the pieces will become too small to work with easily.

Once you have learned the Quick-Strip method, you can apply it to many other paper-piecing patterns. To determine what size strip to cut, place the $\frac{1}{4}$" line of your ruler on the sewing line for a particular area, then measure across the area to the widest point. Add $\frac{1}{2}$" additional seam allowance to this measurement, and cut your strip that size. Measuring this way adds a $\frac{3}{4}$" total seam allowance instead of the standard $\frac{1}{2}$" ($\frac{1}{4}$" for each side), which allows a little extra room in case the paper is not placed at exactly the $\frac{1}{4}$" seam allowance.

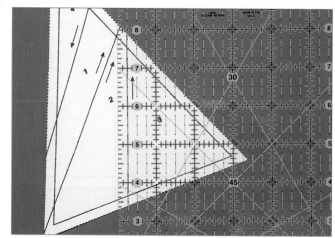

Projects

The following projects are starting points for planning and making your own quilts. Make the projects as they are presented to learn the techniques, then build on the block patterns with your own settings and designs to truly make them your own.

create

Quilt size: 52" x 52"

MIDNIGHT GARDEN

Made by Peggy Martin, 2002
Quilted by Carolyn Reynolds

Spinning Star and Serendipity blocks bordered with a large floral print create the look of a garden at night with whirling flowers and branches reflecting the moonlight. These are two of my favorite blocks because they are so easy to piece using the Quick-Strip Paper-Piecing technique.

Choosing the Fabric

For my Spinning Star blocks I chose assorted hot colors in reds, yellows, oranges, and pinks. I used fabrics that appear as solids for the center star point areas and a larger print in area 3 to create movement. For contrast, I made each of the Serendipity blocks identical.

Fabric Requirements

Five 12" Spinning Star blocks
Four 12" Serendipity blocks

Spinning Star Blocks

5 assorted yellow, red, and orange fabrics for area 1: $1/8$ yard of each

15 assorted yellow, red, and orange fabrics for areas 2, 3, and 4: $1/4$ yard of each

Serendipity Blocks

Red fabric: $3/8$ yard

Orange fabric: $3/8$ yard

Pink fabric: $1/4$ yard

Yellow fabric: $1/4$ yard

Black print fabric for background, inner border, and binding: 2 yards

Large print fabric for outer border: $1^1/4$ yards

Backing: $3^1/8$ yards

Batting: 56" x 56"

Spinning Star

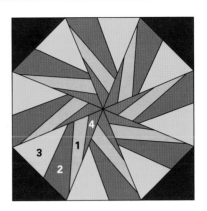

Cutting

Pattern Area	Fabric	Cut
#1	Each of 5 fabrics	2 strips 1 $3/4$"
#2	Each of 5 fabrics	2 strips 2 $1/2$"
#3	Each of 5 fabrics	2 strips 3 $1/2$"
#4	Each of 5 fabrics	2 strips 1 $3/4$"
Corner Triangles	Black print	10 squares 4 $1/2$", then cut once diagonally

Making the Blocks

Make five.

1 Make 40 copies of the Spinning Star pattern on page 30.

2 Referring to Quick-Strip Paper Piecing on page 12 for detailed instructions, paper piece 5 blocks using 8 paper patterns for each block and the strips listed in the chart above.

3 For each block, sew the units together in pairs, then into 2 groups of 4, pressing the seam allowances in the same direction as indicated by the arrows.

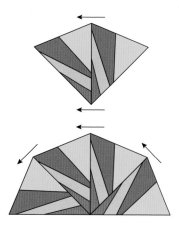

4 Join the 2 halves of the block to make the octagon, and "open out" the center as shown on page 20. Press the seams in a circle, all in the same direction.

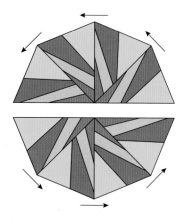

5 Add the background triangles to the 4 corners of each block and press towards the background triangles. Trim corners to square up the blocks to 12 ½".

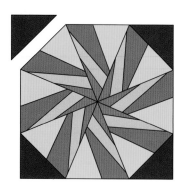

Serendipity

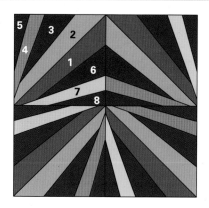

Cutting

Pattern Area	Fabric	Cut
#1	Red	4 strips 2 ¼"
#2	Orange	4 strips 2 ¼"
#3	Black print	3 strips 2 ½"
#4	Pink	4 strips 1 ¾"
#5	Black print	3 strips 1 ¾"
#6	Black print	3 strips 2 ½"
#7	Yellow	4 strips 1 ¾"
#8	Black print	3 strips 1 ¾"

Making the Blocks

Make four.

1 Make 16 copies of the Serendipity pattern on page 31.

2 Referring to the Quick-Strip Paper Piecing on page 12 for detailed instructions, paper-piece all 16 units identically, using the strips listed in the chart on page 28.

3 Arrange and sew the units together in pairs. Press the seams in opposing directions.

4 Join the 2 halves. Press the seam to one side.

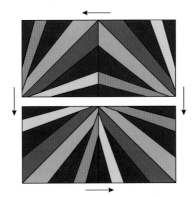

Cutting Borders

Pattern Area	Fabric	Cut
Inner Border	Black print	4 strips 2 1/2"
Outer Border	Large print	5 strips 6 1/2"

Assembly

1 Alternate the Spinning Star blocks and the Serendipity blocks, rotating the Serendipity blocks so they spin around the center as shown in the quilt photo. Sew the blocks into 3 rows, alternating the pressing direction in each row. Sew the rows together and press.

2 Trim 2 of the inner border strips to 36" and sew to the top and bottom of the quilt. Press. Trim 2 inner border strips to 40 1/2" and sew to the sides of the quilt. Press.

3 Trim 2 of the outer border strips to 40 1/2" and sew to the top and bottom of the quilt. Press. Cut 1 outer border strip in half and sew half to each of the remaining outer border strips. Trim to 52 1/2" and sew to the sides of the quilt and press.

Finishing

1 Refer to Layering and Basting on page 104 to put together the quilt, batting, and backing.

2 Since this quilt has a large number of seams, we used an overall pattern of leaves, buds, and vines and a double strand of variegated rayon thread. Refer to Quilting on page 104 for more information.

3 Bind the quilt, referring to Binding on page 104.

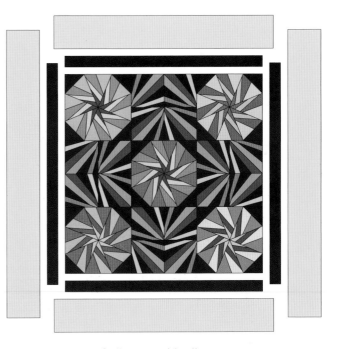

Quilt assembly diagram

Design Options

You can create a variety of exciting quilt designs with the Serendipity block, depending on how you lay them out. Here are just a few of the possibilities.

Queen's X

Fireworks

Pinwheel

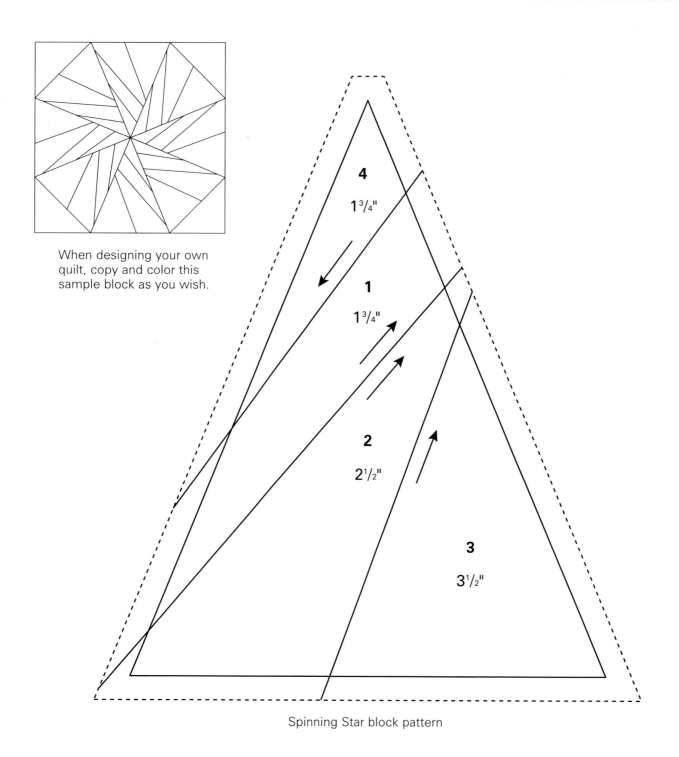

When designing your own quilt, copy and color this sample block as you wish.

4

1³/₄"

1

1³/₄"

2

2¹/₂"

3

3¹/₂"

Spinning Star block pattern

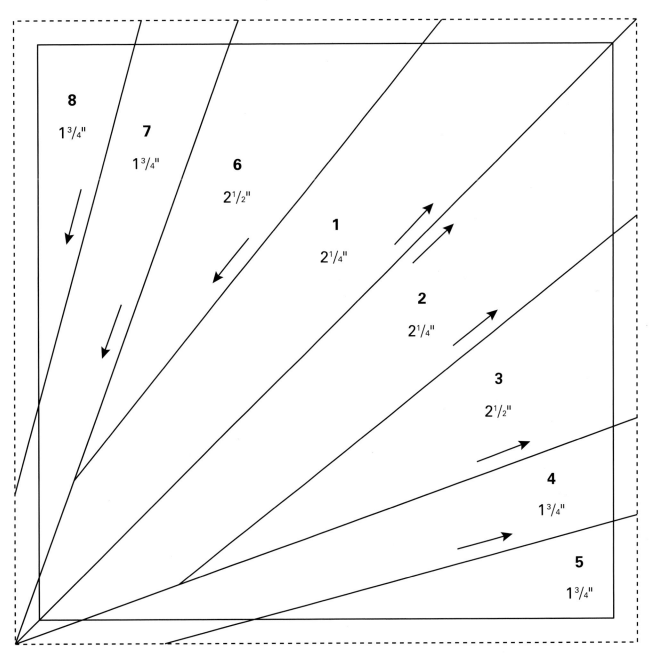

8

$1^{3}/_{4}$"

7

$1^{3}/_{4}$"

6

$2^{1}/_{2}$"

1

$2^{1}/_{4}$"

2

$2^{1}/_{4}$"

3

$2^{1}/_{2}$"

4

$1^{3}/_{4}$"

5

$1^{3}/_{4}$"

Serendipity block pattern

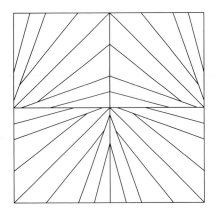

When designing your own quilt, copy and color this sample block as you wish.

More Quilts

Playing with different arrangements of the Serendipity block produces some wonderful designs. Here are two quilts showing two different settings of the block. Note also how differently the blocks are colored to produce completely different-looking quilts, yet they both use the same Serendipity block.

Quilt size: 43" x 43"

THE DAWNING

Made by Peggy Martin, 2002
Quilted by Carolyn Reynolds

Serendipity blocks are shaded from light to dark in jewel tones with hot pink pinwheels floating through. This quilt gives the illusion that the blocks are on point, but they are all straight-set.

Quilt size: 30" x 30"

LIGHT UP THE NIGHT

Made and quilted by Patricia Wolfe, 2002

Serendipity blocks in a Fireworks variation are pieced with bright fabrics on a silver-gray background. Pat embellished the quilt with silver star sequins, and quilted it in swirling patterns with silver metallic threads. The border is an arrangement of the Shrinking Flying Geese.

Quilt size: 26" x 26"

MILLENNIUM STAR

Made and quilted by Peggy Martin, 2002

This block is fast and easy to sew and large enough to stand on its own as a small wallhanging, or make several blocks for a larger quilt. You can easily complete this little quilt in an afternoon.

Choosing the Fabric

I used yellow and green for two of the star points and red and orange for the center star. These could be done using one fabric for adjacent star points and another fabric for the central star for a more solid look (see Christmas Star variation on page 39). Look at the other quilts at the end of this project for more fabric and color ideas.

Fabric Requirements

One 18" Millennium Star block

Black print fabric for background: $\frac{1}{2}$ yard

Bright floral print fabric: $\frac{3}{8}$ yard

Yellow fabric: $\frac{1}{4}$ yard

Medium green fabric: $\frac{1}{8}$ yard

Dark green fabric: $\frac{1}{8}$ yard

Light orange fabric: $\frac{1}{8}$ yard

Red-orange fabric: $\frac{1}{8}$ yard

Print fabric for border: $\frac{1}{2}$ yard

Binding: $\frac{1}{4}$ yard

Backing: $\frac{7}{8}$ yard

Batting: 31" x 31"

Millennium Star

Cutting

Pattern Area	Fabric	Cut
#1	Bright floral print	2 strips 2 $\frac{1}{2}$"
#2 and #3	Yellow	3 strips 2"
#4 and #5	Black print	2 strips 4 $\frac{1}{2}$"
#6	Medium green	2 strips 1 $\frac{1}{2}$"
#7	Dark green	2 strips 1 $\frac{1}{2}$"
#8	Light orange	2 strips 1 $\frac{3}{4}$"
#9	Red-orange	2 strips 2"
Corner Triangles	Black print	2 squares 6 $\frac{1}{2}$", then cut once diagonally
	Border print	3 strips 4 $\frac{1}{2}$"

Making the Blocks

1 Enlarge Millennium Star pattern on page 37 to 125%. Make 8 copies of the enlarged pattern.

2 Referring to Quick-Strip Paper Piecing on page 12 for detailed instructions, paper-piece 8 identical units, using the strips listed in the chart on page 35.

3 Sew the units together in pairs, then into 2 groups of 4, pressing all the seams in the same direction.

4 Join the 2 halves of the block, and "open out" the center as shown on page 20. Press the seams in a circle, all in the same direction.

5 Add the corner triangles, and press toward the triangles. Trim corners to square up the block to $18\frac{1}{2}$".

Assembling the Quilt

1 Cut 1 border strip into 2 strips, each $18\frac{1}{2}$", and sew to the top and bottom of the quilt. Press.

2 Trim 2 border strips to $26\frac{1}{2}$" and sew to the sides of the quilt. Press.

Finishing

1 Refer to Layering and Basting on page 104 to put together the quilt, batting, and backing.

2 I quilted in-the-ditch around the star points, then added free-form flame shapes in the larger print and background areas and swirls in the borders. Refer to Quilting on page 104 for more information.

3 Bind the quilt, referring to Binding on page 104.

Quilt assembly diagram

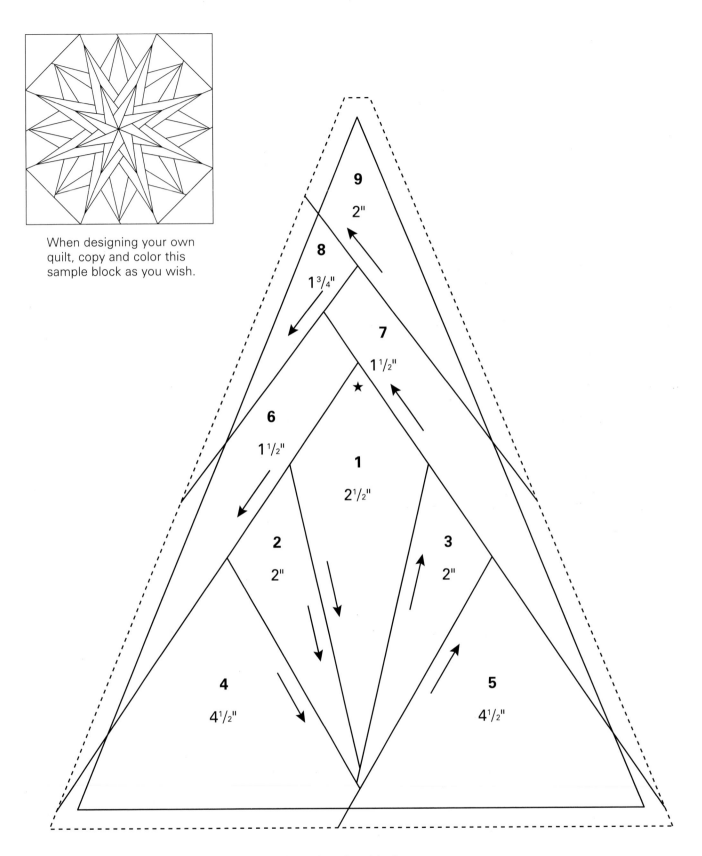

When designing your own
quilt, copy and color this
sample block as you wish.

9

2"

8

1³/₄"

7

1¹/₂"

★

6

1¹/₂"

1

2¹/₂"

2

2"

3

2"

4

4¹/₂"

5

4¹/₂"

Millennium Star block pattern

Enlarge 125% and make 8 copies.

★ Be sure to allow enough fabric on strip to cover this point when piecing and trimming.

More Quilts

It is amazing how different this quilt can look, simply done in a different color scheme. To show you how the look can change, I've made three other versions of the *Millennium Star* quilt using different color schemes.

Quilt size: 26" x 26"

GEMSTAR

Made and quilted by Peggy Martin, 2001

CHRISTMAS STAR

Made by Peggy Martin, 2001

Quilt size: 26" x 26"

WATERMELON STAR

Made by Peggy Martin, 2001

Quilt size: 26" x 26"

Quilt size: 62" x 62"

NEW YORK BEAUTY

Made by Peggy Martin, 2002
Quilted by Wendy Knight

The golds, greens, and burgundies are reminiscent of autumn days
when leaves are just beginning to turn, but summer's heat still lingers
for a few more days. This traditional block used to be considered
difficult, but it is amazingly fast to piece using Quick-Strip Paper
Piecing and invisible machine appliqué for the curved seams.

Choosing the Fabric

I was inspired to make this quilt by a great sunflower batik fabric with shades of yellows, golds, oranges, greens, and burgundies. From this color palette, I selected yellows and golds for the backgrounds of the New York Beauty pieced arcs and deep burgundies and greens for the points in the arcs. Having a strong contrast in the point section really helps the points to stand out. I added oranges, greens, and browns in the backgrounds plus a final border using that great sunflower fabric.

Fabric Requirements

Thirty-six 6" New York Beauty blocks

Assorted dark greens and burgundies: 2 yards total (1 yard for pattern A and 1 yard for border points)

Assorted yellows and golds: 3 yards total (1$\frac{3}{4}$ yards for pattern A and 1$\frac{1}{4}$ yards for pieced border).

Assorted green, orange, and rust prints for patterns B and C (setting pieces): 1$\frac{1}{2}$ yards total

Burgundy for accent borders and binding: 1$\frac{1}{2}$ yards

Burgundy, green, and gold print for outer border: 1$\frac{1}{8}$ yard

Backing: 3$\frac{3}{4}$ yards

Batting: 66" x 66"

Freezer paper for appliqué

Washable fabric glue stick (for appliqué basting methods 1 and 3)

Spray starch (for appliqué basting method 2)

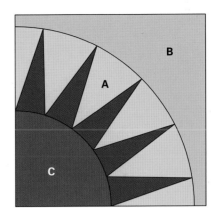

Cutting

Pattern Area	Fabric	Cut
Pattern A points (even numbers)	Assorted dark greens and burgundies	18 strips 1$\frac{3}{4}$"
Pattern A backgrounds (odd numbers)	Assorted yellows and golds	20 strips 2$\frac{1}{2}$"
Pattern B	Assorted green, orange, and rust prints	4 strips 6$\frac{1}{2}$" or equivalent scraps
Pattern C	Assorted green, orange, and rust prints	4 strips 3$\frac{1}{2}$" or equivalent scraps

*TIP

I pieced 4 blocks at a time, using 2 strips of the same green or burgundy fabric and 2 strips of the same yellow to make 4 blocks. For a scrappier quilt, switch to different fabric strips for each step, giving more variety to the points and backgrounds.

Making the Blocks

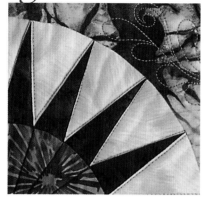

1 Make 36 copies of New York Beauty pattern A on page 46. Make 9 copies of patterns B and C on page 47. Staple each of the 9 copies of patterns B and C to 4 layers of freezer paper, then cut on the outer lines to make 36 freezer paper patterns for appliqué basting of B and C.

2 Referring to Quick-Strip Paper Piecing on page 12 for detailed instructions, paper piece 36 pattern A units using the strips indicated in the chart on page 41.

3 Press the shiny side of freezer paper patterns B and C to the wrong sides of the $6\frac{1}{2}$"-wide and $3\frac{1}{2}$"-wide fabric strips, placing a straight edge of the pattern along the grainline of the fabric. Leave enough room between each pattern to add $\frac{1}{4}$" seam allowance to each curved edge. Cut out 36 pattern B's and 36 pattern C's, adding a $\frac{1}{4}$" seam allowance to the curved edges, as indicated on the pattern.

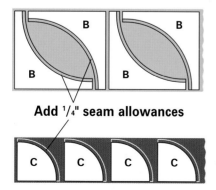

Add $\frac{1}{4}$" seam allowances

Making the Appliqué Blocks

Three different methods of basting the edges of the appliqué blocks are given below. You might want to experiment to see which method you prefer. For all methods, the curve on pattern B must be clipped every inch or so in order to turn it under. It is not necessary to clip the curve on pattern C.

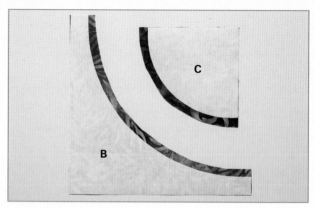

Method 1: Glue basting

1. After cutting the pieces including the seam allowances, leave the freezer paper pattern in place on the wrong side of the fabric.

2. Working on a paper towel or paper plate to protect your work surface, spread washable fabric glue stick on the fabric seam allowance of the curved edges of patterns B and C.

3. Fold the fabric over the curved edge of the freezer paper pattern and smooth down with your fingers.

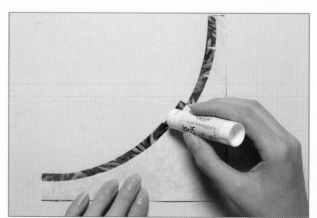

Method 2: Starch basting

1. After cutting the pieces, including the seam allowances, leave the freezer paper pattern in place on the wrong side of the fabric.

2. Cover your ironing surface with a press cloth. Spray a small amount of spray starch into the cap of the spray starch can. Using a small stencil brush or a cotton swab, dab starch onto the curved seam allowance of the fabric.

3. Using your fingers or a stiletto to fold the seam allowance over the curved edge of the freezer paper pattern, press the fabric seam allowance onto the freezer paper. Hold the iron in place until the starch is dried and set.

Method 3: Pressing to freezer paper

1. After cutting the pieces, including the seam allowances, remove the freezer paper pattern from the wrong side of the fabric.

2. Turn the freezer paper pattern over and place on the wrong side of the fabric pieces with the shiny side up. Align the straight edges of the paper with the straight edges of the fabric pieces.

3. Place a few spots of glue stick in the corners of the paper to hold it in place on the fabric. Use your fingers or a stiletto to fold the seam allowance over the curved edge of the freezer paper pattern. Press the fabric seam allowance onto the shiny side of the freezer paper using a hot iron with no steam.

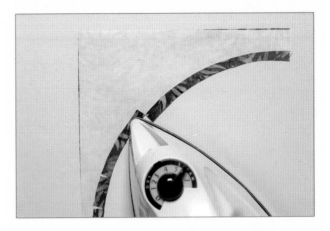

Machine Appliqué

After you have basted under the curved edges of the arcs, machine appliqué them in position according to the following steps.

1. Place B and C on top of paper-pieced arc A. Baste in place with a few spots of glue stick on the seam allowance.

2. Thread your sewing machine with monofilament nylon thread and put the same monofilament or a neutral cotton thread in the bobbin. Lower the top tension slightly, and use a size 75/11 quilting or jeans/denim needle.

3. Set your machine to a blind-hem stitch with a very small stitch length (.5 to 1) and a very narrow zigzag (.5 to 1). The straight part of the stitch falls on the paper-pieced arc A very near to the folded edge of B or C. The narrow zigzag will just catch the basted fold of B or C.

Blind hem stitch

Cutting Pieced and Solid Borders

Pattern Area	Fabric	Cut
Points (even numbers)	Assorted dark greens and burgundies	10 strips $2\frac{3}{4}$"
Background (odd numbers)	Assorted yellows and golds	13 strips $2\frac{3}{4}$"
Area 1 of border corners	Burgundy	1 strip $2\frac{3}{4}$"
Areas 2 and 3 of border corners	Yellow or gold	2 strips 3"
First and third narrow accent borders	Burgundy	12 strips $2\frac{1}{2}$"
Outer border	Burgundy, green, and gold print	6 strips $5\frac{1}{2}$"

Making the Paper-Pieced Borders

1 Make 20 copies of the border strip pattern on page 48 and 4 copies of the border corner pattern on page 49.

2 Referring to page 22 for detailed instructions, paper-piece the borders, using the strips listed in the chart. Piece together 5 border strips end to end to make each of the 4 border segments. Each border strip will have a total of 20 points when completed.

3 Referring to Quick-Strip Paper Piecing on page 12 for detailed instructions, paper piece the 4 border corners.

Assembling the Quilt

1 Arrange the New York Beauty blocks as shown in the quilt photo. Sew the blocks into 6 rows, alternating the pressing direction in each row. Sew the rows together and press.

2 Trim 2 narrow accent border strips to $36\frac{1}{2}$" and sew to the top and bottom of the quilt. Press toward the accent border. Trim 2 narrow accent border strips to $40\frac{1}{2}$" and sew to the sides of the quilt. Press toward the accent border.

3 Sew 2 of the paper-pieced borders to the top and bottom of the quilt. Press.

4 Sew a paper-pieced border corner to each end of the 2 remaining paper-pieced borders. Sew to the sides of the quilt. Press toward the accent border.

5 Cut 2 narrow accent border strips in half and sew half to each of the remaining accent border strips. Trim 2 of the narrow accent border strips to $48\frac{1}{2}$" and sew to the top and bottom of the quilt. Press. Trim 2 inner narrow accent border strips to $52\frac{1}{2}$" and sew to the sides of the quilt. Press toward the accent border.

6 Cut 2 outer border strips in half and sew half to each of the remaining outer border strips. Press toward the accent border. Trim 2 of the outer border strips to 52½" and sew to the top and bottom of the quilt. Trim 2 outer border strips to 62½" and sew to the sides of the quilt and press toward the accent border.

Finishing

1 Refer to Layering and Basting on page 104 to put together the quilt, batting, and backing.

2 This quilt was stitched-in-the-ditch around the points, then quilted with vines and feathers in the larger areas and borders. Refer to Quilting on page 104 for more information.

3 Bind the quilt, referring to Binding on page 104.

Quilt assembly diagram

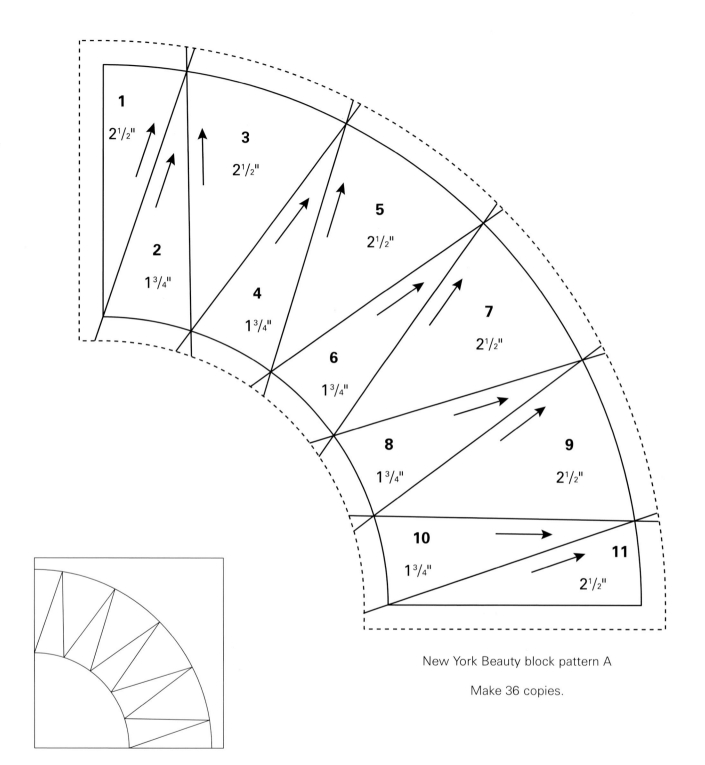

1
2½"

2
1¾"

3
2½"

4
1¾"

5
2½"

6
1¾"

7
2½"

8
1¾"

9
2½"

10
1¾"

11
2½"

New York Beauty block pattern A

Make 36 copies.

When designing your own
quilt, copy and color this
sample block as you wish.

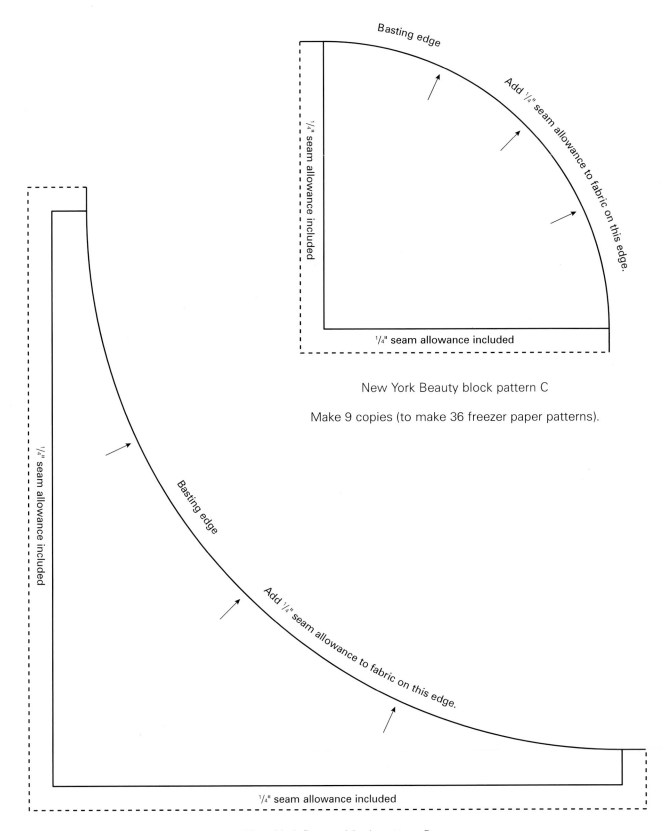

Basting edge

Add 1/4" seam allowance to fabric on this edge.

1/4" seam allowance included

1/4" seam allowance included

New York Beauty block pattern C

Make 9 copies (to make 36 freezer paper patterns).

Basting edge

Add 1/4" seam allowance to fabric on this edge.

1/4" seam allowance included

1/4" seam allowance included

New York Beauty block pattern B

Make 9 copies (to make 36 freezer paper patterns).

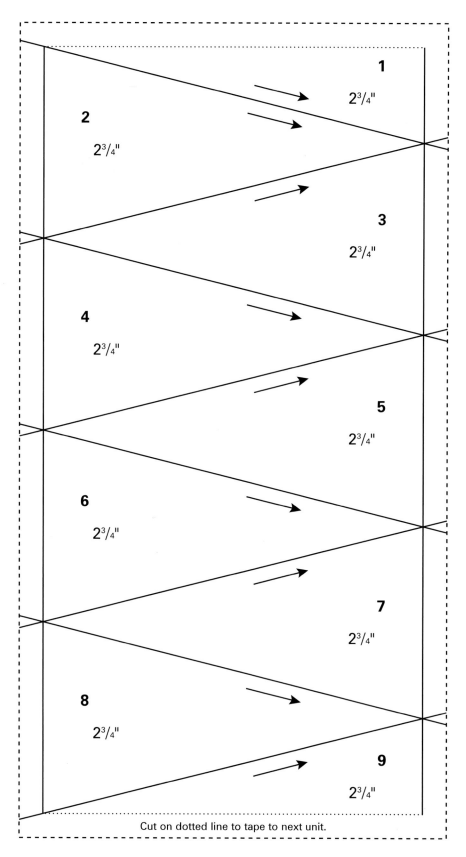

Cut on dotted line to tape to next unit.

New York Beauty border strip

Make 20 copies.

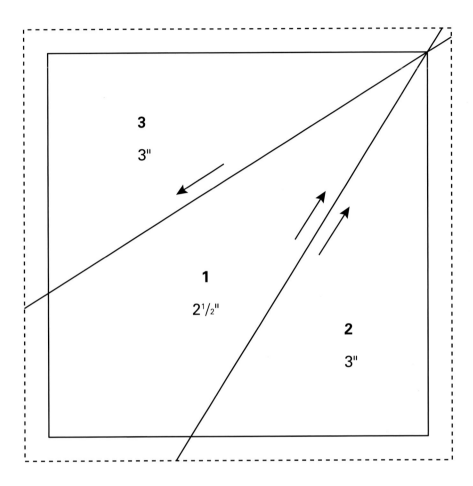

New York Beauty border corner

Make 4 copies.

More Quilts

There are many other ways to lay out the New York Beauty blocks. Playing with these blocks is similar to playing with Log Cabin blocks. Try turning the blocks to create your own symmetrical or asymmetrical designs before you assemble your quilt.

Quilt size: 28" x 28"

CENTER OF ATTENTION

Made and quilted by Lorraine Marstall, 2002

Sixteen New York Beauty blocks, set in a barn-raising design, positively glow with color in this lively wall quilt.

Quilt size: 29" x 29"

SUMMER DELIGHTS

Made and quilted by Jean Nagy, 2002

Jean was inspired by the watermelon fabric to make this whimsical New York Beauty quilt. And what picnic is complete without ants? Jean hand-sewed plastic ants working their way across this truly delightful quilt!

Quilt size: 86" x 86"

RAINBOW GALAXY

Made by Peggy Martin, 2000
Quilted by Lisa Taylor

Bright, rainbow-colored stars and pinwheels sparkle against a dark
blue-violet background in this dramatic sampler quilt. The Flying
Geese border is easy to piece using the Quick-Strip Paper-Piecing
method and is a perfect finishing touch to this collection of star-
shaped blocks.

Choosing the Fabric

For some time I'd wanted to do a quilt with a deep purple background, and I decided this was the one. For the stars I chose bright, hot colors like yellows, reds, oranges, and pinks that would really stand out, and sometimes even vibrate, against the dark background of deep blue-violet. Then I added in greens and bright blues for accents. I liked the idea of playing with stripes using the Quick-Strip Paper-Piecing method, so I used at least one striped fabric in each paper-pieced block. The royal blue fabric in the Stepping Stones blocks came from that time-honored quilting tradition . . . I simply ran out of fabric! I think adding it in made the quilt much more interesting.

Fabric Requirements

Thirteen 12" Star blocks with borders added to make 14" blocks

Twelve 14" Stepping Stone blocks

Mottled dark blue-violet for background and binding: 7 yards

Bright yellows, oranges, reds, pinks, blues, greens, turquoises for star points, Stepping Stones blocks, and Flying Geese border: 1 yard *each* of at least 6–8 fabrics. *For a scrappier version, select at least ¹/₄ yard each of many fabrics to total 6–8 yards.*

Mottled royal blue for Stepping Stones blocks: 1¹/₂ yards

Yellow/orange for inner border: ⁵/₈ yard

Backing: 7¹/₂ yards

Batting: 91" x 91"

Quick-Strip Paper-Pieced Blocks

Make one each of the following block patterns. Each pattern has a color picture to give you ideas for colors, and a lined sketch of the block for you to trace or copy to try your own colorations. The lined sketches are found with the patterns beginning on page 70.

Simple Star

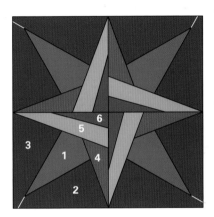

12" Simple Star block

Cutting

Pattern Area	Fabric	Cut
#1	Multi-stripe	1 strip 3 ¹/₄"
#2	Dark blue-violet	1 strip 4"
#3	Dark blue-violet	1 strip 4"
#4	Red	1 strip 2"
#5	Orange	1 strip 2"
#6	Purple	1 strip 1³/₄"

Making the Block

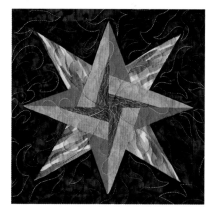

1 Make 4 copies of the Simple Star pattern on page 73.

2 Referring to Quick-Strip Paper Piecing on page 12 for detailed instructions, paper-piece 4 identical units, using the strips listed in the chart on page 53.

3 Sew the units together in pairs, rotating the units as shown in the photo. Press the seams in opposing directions.

4 Join the 2 halves of the block, and press the seam to one side.

Stargaze

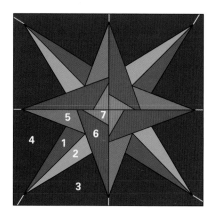

12" Stargaze block

Cutting

Pattern Area	Fabric	Cut
#1	Green and purple print	1 strip 2"
#2	Green print	1 strip 2"
#3	Dark blue-violet	1 strip 4¹/₄"
#4	Dark blue-violet	1 strip 4¹/₄"
#5	Light green	1 strip 2"
#6	Stripe	1 strip 2¹/₂"
#7	Pink	1 strip 1³/₄"

Making the Block

1 Make 4 copies of the Stargaze pattern on page 74.

2 Referring to Quick-Strip Paper Piecing on page 12 for detailed instructions, paper-piece 4 identical units, using the strips listed in the above chart.

3 Sew the units together in pairs, rotating the units as shown in the photo. Press the seams in opposing directions.

4 Join the 2 halves of the block, and press the seam to one side.

Faceted Star

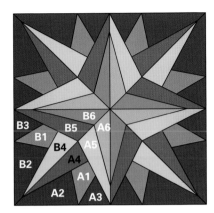

12" Faceted Star block

Cutting

Pattern Area	Fabric	Cut
Patterns A and B #1	Yellow stripe	1 strip 2¼"
Patterns A and B #2	Dark blue-violet	1 strip 4¾"
Patterns A and B #3	Dark blue-violet	1 strip 2½"
Pattern A #4	Red	1 strip 2¼"
Pattern A #5	Yellow/gold	1 strip 2¼"
Pattern A #6	Turquoise stripe	1 strip 2"
Pattern B #4	Yellow	1 strip 2¼"
Pattern B #5	Red	1 strip 2¼"
Pattern B #6	Turquoise	1 strip 2"

Making the Block

1 Make 4 copies of Faceted Star Pattern A and 4 copies of Faceted Star Pattern B on page 75.

2 Referring to Quick-Strip Paper Piecing on page 12 for detailed instructions, paper-piece 4 identical A units and 4 identical B units, using the strips listed in the chart. Do all A's first, then all B's to avoid confusion.

3 Sew together A and B to make 4 squares. Press the seams to the left.

4 Rotate the 4 squares as shown in the photo above and sew together. Press seams in opposing directions.

5 Join the 2 halves of the block, and "open out" the center as shown on page 20. Press the seams in a circle, all in the same direction.

Uneven Star

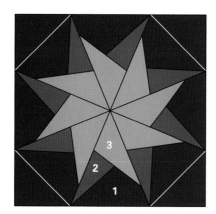

12" Uneven Star block

Cutting

Pattern Area	Fabric	Cut
#1	Dark blue-violet	1 strip 4$\frac{1}{4}$"
#2	Red-orange	1 strip 2$\frac{1}{2}$"
#3	Red-orange stripe	1 strip 3$\frac{1}{2}$"
Corner triangles	Dark blue-violet	2 squares 4$\frac{1}{2}$", then cut once diagonally

Making the Block

1 Make 8 copies of the Uneven Star pattern on page 76.

2 Referring to Quick-Strip Paper Piecing on page 12 for detailed instructions, paper-piece 8 identical units, using the strips listed in the chart.

3 Sew the units together in pairs, then into 2 groups of 4, pressing the seams in the same direction.

4 Join the 2 halves of the block, and "open out" the center as shown on page 20. Press the seams in a circle, all in the same direction.

5 Add the corner triangles, and press toward the triangles. Trim corners to square up the block to 12$\frac{1}{2}$".

Twisted Star

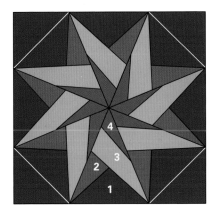

12" Twisted Star block

Cutting

Pattern Area	Fabric	Cut
#1	Dark blue-violet	1 strip 4¼"
#2	Red-orange	1 strip 2½"
#3	Stripe	2 strips 2¼"
#4	Green	1 strip 2"
Corner triangles	Dark blue-violet	2 squares 4½", then cut once diagonally

Making the Block

1 Make 8 copies of the Twisted Star pattern on page 77.

2 Referring to Quick-Strip Paper Piecing on page 12 for detailed instructions, paper-piece 8 identical units, using the strips listed in the chart.

3 Sew the units together in pairs, then into 2 groups of 4, pressing the seams in the same direction.

4 Join the 2 halves of the block, and "open out" the center as shown on page 20. Press the seams in a circle, all in the same direction.

5 Add the corner triangles, and press toward the triangles. Trim corners to square up the block to 12½".

Whirling Star

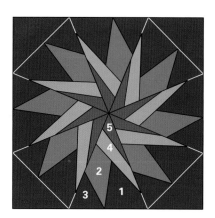

12" Whirling Star block

Cutting

Pattern Area	Fabric	Cut
#1	Dark blue-violet	1 strip 3$^{1}/_{2}$"
#2	Turquoise stripe	1 strip 2$^{1}/_{2}$"
#3	Dark blue-violet	2 strips 2$^{3}/_{4}$"
#4	Turquoise	2 strips 1$^{3}/_{4}$"
#5	Red	2 strips 1$^{3}/_{4}$"
Corner triangles	Dark blue-violet	2 squares 4$^{1}/_{2}$", then cut once diagonally

Making the Block

1 Make 8 copies of the Whirling Star pattern on page 78.

2 Referring to Quick-Strip Paper Piecing on page 12 for detailed instructions, paper-piece 8 identical units, using the strips listed in the chart.

3 Sew the units together in pairs, then into 2 groups of 4, pressing the seams in the same direction.

4 Join the 2 halves of the block, and "open out" the center as shown on page 20. Press the seams in a circle, all in the same direction.

5 Add the corner triangles, and press toward the triangles. Trim corners to square up the block to 12$^{1}/_{2}$".

Whirligig

2" Whirligig block

Cutting

Pattern Area	Fabric	Cut
#1	Pink and purple stripe	1 strip 1¾"
#2	Pink	1 strip 1¾"
#3	Dark blue-violet	1 strip 2¾"
#4	Dark blue-violet	1 strip 2"
#5	Green print	2 strips 2¼"
#6	Green and purple print	2 strips 1¾"
#7	Green	2 strips 1¾"
Corner triangles	Dark blue-violet	2 squares 4½", then cut once diagonally

Making the Block

1 Make 8 copies of the Whirligig pattern on page 79.

2 Referring to Quick-Strip Paper Piecing on page 12 for detailed instructions, paper-piece 8 identical units, using the strips listed in the chart.

3 Sew the units together in pairs, then into 2 groups of 4, pressing the seams in the same direction.

4 Join the 2 halves of the block, and "open out" the center as shown on page 20. Press the seams in a circle, all the same direction.

5 Add the corner triangles, and press toward the triangles. Trim corners to square up the block to 12½".

Starburst

12" Starburst block

Cutting

Pattern Area	Fabric	Cut
#1	Yellow stripe	1 strip 2"
#2	Red stripe	1 strip 2"
#3	Dark blue-violet	1 strip 3¼"
#4	Dark blue-violet	1 strip 3¼"
#5	Red	1 strip 1½"
#6	Yellow	2 strips 2"
Corner triangles	Dark blue-violet	2 squares 4½", then cut once diagonally

Making the Block

1 Make 8 copies of the Starburst pattern on page 80.

2 Referring to Quick-Strip Paper Piecing on page 12 for detailed instructions, paper-piece 8 identical units, using the strips listed in the chart.

3 Sew the units together in pairs, then into 2 groups of 4, pressing the seams in the same direction.

4 Join the 2 halves of the block, and "open out" the center as shown on page 20. Press the seams in a circle, all in the same direction.

5 Add the corner triangles, and press toward the triangles. Trim corners to square up the block to 12½".

Radiant Star

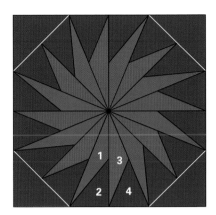

12" Radiant Star block

Cutting

Pattern Area	Fabric	Cut
#1	Stripe	2 strips 2³/₄"
#2	Dark blue-violet	2 strips 2³/₄"
#3	Red	2 strips 2"
#4	Dark blue-violet	1 strip 3¹/₄"
Corner triangles	Dark blue-violet	2 squares 4¹/₂", then cut once diagonally

Making the Block

1 Make 8 copies of the Radiant Star pattern on page 81.

2 Referring to Quick-Strip Paper Piecing on page 12 for detailed instructions, paper-piece 8 identical units, using the strips listed in the chart.

3 Sew the units together in pairs, then into 2 groups of 4, pressing the seams in the same direction.

4 Join the 2 halves of the block, and "open out" the center as shown on page 20. Press the seams in a circle, all in the same direction.

5 Add the corner triangles, and press toward the triangles. Trim corners to square up the block to 12¹/₂".

Cattywampus Star

12" Cattywampus Star block

Cutting

Pattern Area	Fabric	Cut
#1	Yellow	1 strip 2"
#2	Dark blue-violet	1 strip 3$\frac{1}{2}$"
#3	Red	1 strip 1$\frac{3}{4}$"
#4	Dark blue-violet	1 strip 3$\frac{1}{2}$"
#5	Stripe	2 strips 2$\frac{3}{4}$"
Corner triangles	Dark blue-violet	2 squares 4$\frac{1}{2}$", then cut once diagonally

Making the Block

1 Make 8 copies of the Cattywampus Star pattern on page 82.

2 Referring to Quick-Strip Paper Piecing on page 12 for detailed instructions, paper-piece 8 identical units, using the strips listed in the chart.

3 Sew the units together in pairs, then into 2 groups of 4, pressing the seams in the same direction.

4 Join the 2 halves of the block, and "open out" the center as shown on page 20. Press the seams in a circle, all in the same direction.

5 Add the corner triangles, and press toward the triangles. Trim corners to square up the block to 12$\frac{1}{2}$".

Super Star

12" Super Star block

Cutting

Pattern Area	Fabric	Cut
#1	Red	1 strip 1½"
#2	Yellow	1 strip 1½"
#3	Dark blue-violet	1 strip 3¼"
#4	Dark blue-violet	1 strip 3¼"
#5	Stripe	1 strip 1¾"
#6	Stripe	2 strips 1¾"
#7	Green	1 strip 1¼"
#8	Green	1 strip 1¼"
#9	Yellow	1 strip 1¼"
#10	Red	1 strip 1¾"
Corner triangles	Dark blue-violet	2 squares 4½", then cut once diagonally

Making the Block

1 Make 8 copies of the Super Star pattern on page 83.

2 Referring to Quick-Strip Paper Piecing on page 12 for detailed instructions, paper-piece 8 identical units, using the strips listed in the chart.

3 Sew the units together in pairs, then into 2 groups of 4, pressing the seams in the same direction.

4 Join the 2 halves of the block, and "open out" the center as shown on page 20. Press the seams in a circle, all in the same direction.

5 Add the corner triangles, and press toward the triangles. Trim corners to square up the block to 12½".

Blazing Star

12" Blazing Star block

Cutting

Pattern Area	Fabric	Cut
Unit A #1	Orange stripe	1 strip 1³/₄"
Unit A #2	Dark blue-violet	1 strip 2¹/₂"
Unit A #3	Dark blue-violet	1 strip 2¹/₄"
Unit A #4	Dark green	2 strips 1³/₄"
Unit A #5	Yellow	2 strips 1³/₄"
Unit B #1	Orange stripe	1 strip 1³/₄"
Unit B #2	Dark blue-violet	1 strip 2¹/₂"
Unit B #3	Dark blue-violet	1 strip 2¹/₄"
Unit B #4	Light green	2 strips 1³/₄"
Unit B #5	Orange	2 strips 1³/₄"
Corner triangles	Dark blue-violet	2 squares 4¹/₂", then cut once diagonally

Making the Block

1 Make 8 copies of the Blazing Star unit A pattern and 8 copies of the Blazing Star unit B pattern on page 84.

2 Referring to Quick-Strip Paper Piecing on page 12 for detailed instructions, paper-piece 8 A units and 8 B units, using the strips listed in the chart. Do all A's first, then all B's to avoid confusion.

3 Sew the A and B units together in pairs to make 8 wedges. Sew the wedges into 2 groups of 4. This block has a lot of seam allowances coming together, so you might want to press the construction seams open.

4 Join the 2 halves of the block, and "open out" the center as shown on page 20. Press the seams in a circle, all in the same direction.

5 Add the corner triangles, and press toward the triangles. Trim corners to square up the block to 12¹/₂".

Dutch Star

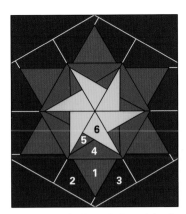

12" x 10³/₈" Dutch Star block

Cutting

Pattern Area	Fabric	Cut
#1	Orange	1 strip 3¹/₄"
#2	Dark blue-violet	1 strip 2¹/₂"
#3	Dark blue-violet	1 strip 2¹/₂"
#4	Stripe	1 strip 2"
#5	Red	1 strip 1¹/₂"
#6	Yellow	1 strip 2¹/₂"
Corner triangles*	Dark blue-violet	Cut 2 and 2 reversed

Use Corner Triangle pattern on page 85.

Making the Block

1   Make 6 copies of the Dutch Star pattern and 1 copy of the Corner Triangle pattern on page 85.

2   Referring to Quick-Strip Paper Piecing on page 12 for detailed instructions, paper-piece 6 identical units, using the strips listed in the chart.

3   Sew the units together in pairs, pressing the seams in the same direction. Add the third unit to each pair to make the 2 halves of the block. If the paper in the seam allowances is becoming too bulky to press flat, carefully remove it.

4   Join the 2 halves to complete the hexagon. Press the seam to one side.

5   Add the corner triangles cut from the template, and press toward the triangles to make the rectangular block.

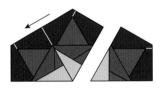

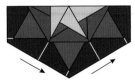

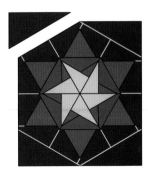

Completing the Star Blocks

Note: You will need to add background strips to each of the star blocks so that they will finish 14" to match the 14" Stepping Stones blocks.

1 Cut 21 strips 1½" wide of background fabric. Cut these into 24 strips 1½" x 12½" and 26 strips 1½" x 14½" (set aside 2 for the Dutch Star).

2 Sew 1½" x 12½" strips to the sides of the star blocks except the Dutch Star. Press toward the strips.

3 Sew 1½" x 14½" strips to the tops and bottoms of the star blocks except the Dutch Star. Press toward the strips.

4 For the Dutch Star block, cut 1 strip 2½" wide of background fabric; cut into 2 strips 2½" x 12½".

5 Sew the 2½"-wide strips to the two narrower sides of the block. Press toward the strips. Taking care to center the star, trim the block to measure 14½" across.

6 Add the remaining 1½" x 14½" strips to the top and bottom of Dutch Star block. Press toward the strips.

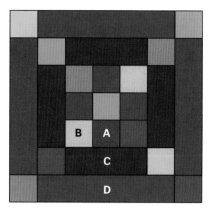

14" Stepping Stones block
Make 12 blocks.

Cutting

Pattern Area	Fabric	Cut
A	Mottled blue	3 strips 2½", then cut into 48 squares 2½"
B	Assorted bright yellow-oranges oranges, and reds	Total of 10 strips 2½", then cut into 156 squares 2½"
C	Dark blue-violet	8 strips 2½", then cut into 48 rectangles 2½" x 6½"
D	Mottled blue	16 strips 2½", then cut into 48 rectangles 2½" x 10½"

Making the Stepping Stones Blocks

1 For the centers of the Stepping Stones blocks, make 12 nine-patch units, using 4 A squares and 5 B squares each.

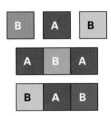

2 Sew a C rectangle to 2 opposite sides of each of the nine-patch units. Press toward C. Sew 2 B squares to the ends of the remaining 24 C rectangles. Press toward C. Sew these sections to the remaining sides of each block and press toward B/C unit.

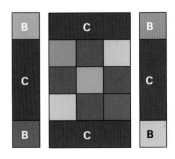

Add C rectangles.

3 Sew a D rectangle to two opposite sides of the block. Press toward D. Sew 2 B squares to the ends of the remaining 24 D rectangles. Press toward D. Sew these sections to the remaining sides of each block and press toward B/D unit.

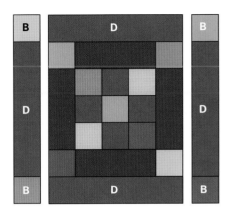

Add D rectangles.

Cutting Pieced Border

For Two 6" Simple Star Blocks

Pattern Area	Fabric	Cut
#1	Stripe	1 strip 2"
#2	Dark blue-violet	1 strip 2½"
#3	Dark blue-violet	1 strip 2½"
#4	Orange	1 strip 1½"
#5	Red	1 strip 1¼"
#6	Yellow	1 strip 1¼"

Cutting for Flying Geese Border and Accent Border:

Pattern Area	Fabric	Cut
Units A & B #1	Assorted reds and oranges	2 strips 3¾"
Units A & B	All remaining areas assorted reds and oranges	8 strips 2¾"
Unit A	Dark blue-violet	10 strips 2¼"
Unit B	Dark blue-violet	2 strips 2¼" 1 strip 2" 1 strip 1½"
Narrow side strips for Flying Geese border	Dark blue-violet	8 strips 1½"
Border strips	Dark blue-violet	6 strips 6½"
Inner accent border	Yellow-orange	8 strips 2½"

Making the Paper-Pieced Border

1 Make 8 copies of the 6" Simple Star pattern on page 70; make 12 copies of Regular Flying Geese pattern A on page 70; make 4 copies of Shrinking Flying Geese pattern B on page 71.

2 Referring to Quick-Strip Paper Piecing on page 12 for detailed instructions and using the strips listed in the above chart, paper-piece two 6" Simple Stars.

3 Referring to page 22 for detailed instructions and using the strips listed in the chart above, paper-piece 12 Flying Geese pattern A units and 4 Flying Geese pattern B units.

4 Sew 3 Regular Flying Geese A strips together end to end into 4 long A border units, with 12 geese each. Sew a Shrinking Flying Geese B unit to an end of each long A border unit to make 4 Flying Geese border units.

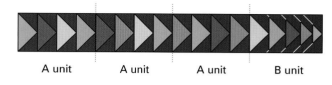

A unit   A unit   A unit   B unit

Flying Geese rows

5 Trim narrow side strips to 32". Sew a strip to either side of each Flying Geese border unit, to make units that measure 6½" x 32". Press toward the strips.

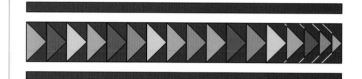

6 Cut 2 border strips in half and sew to remaining border strips. Trim 2 strips to 43" and add to 1 end of 2 Flying Geese border units. Press toward the strip.

7 Trim the 2 remaining border strips to 49". Add the two 6" Simple Stars to 1 end of each of the remaining Flying Geese border units and a strip to the other end. Press toward the strip.

Assembling the Quilt

1 Alternate paper-pieced blocks with Stepping Stones blocks, as shown in the quilt photo and diagram below. Sew the blocks into rows, alternating the pressing direction in each row. Sew the rows together and press.

2 Sew accent border strips together in pairs end to end. Trim 2 of the strips to $70^{1}/_{2}$" and sew to the top and bottom of the quilt. Press toward the borders. Trim 2 of the strips to $74^{1}/_{2}$" and sew to the sides of the quilt. Press.

3 Sew the shorter Flying Geese borders to the top and bottom of the quilt. Press toward the accent border.

4 Sew the longer Flying Geese borders to the sides of the quilt. Press toward the accent border.

Finishing

1 Refer to Layering and Basting on page 104 to put together the quilt, batting, and backing.

2 Each block was quilted with its own individual design and then swirls and flames were quilted in the open areas. Refer to Quilting on page 104 for more information.

3 Bind the quilt, referring to Binding on page 104.

Quilt assembly diagram

Design Options

Try setting your sampler blocks with an alternating Serendipity setting block, in either the Queen's X or Fireworks arrangement. Or choose one of the 12" blocks and alternate it with Stepping Stones blocks for a two-block quilt. Select one of the 12" blocks and base a quilt on it, setting it with sashing or on point for more traditional sets. Look at the gallery section for other quilts based on these blocks.

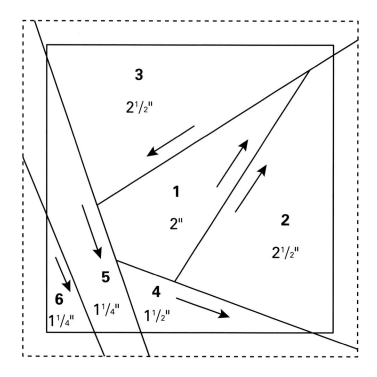

6" Simple Star pattern

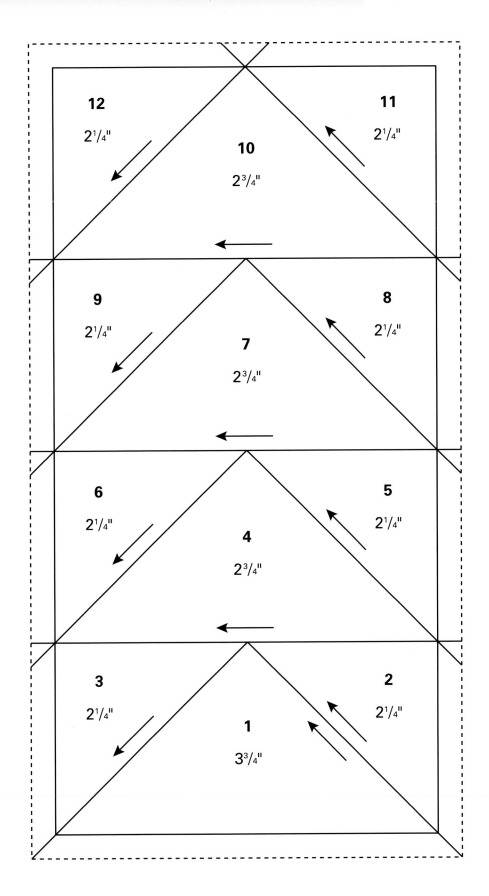

Regular Flying Geese pattern A

Make 12 copies.

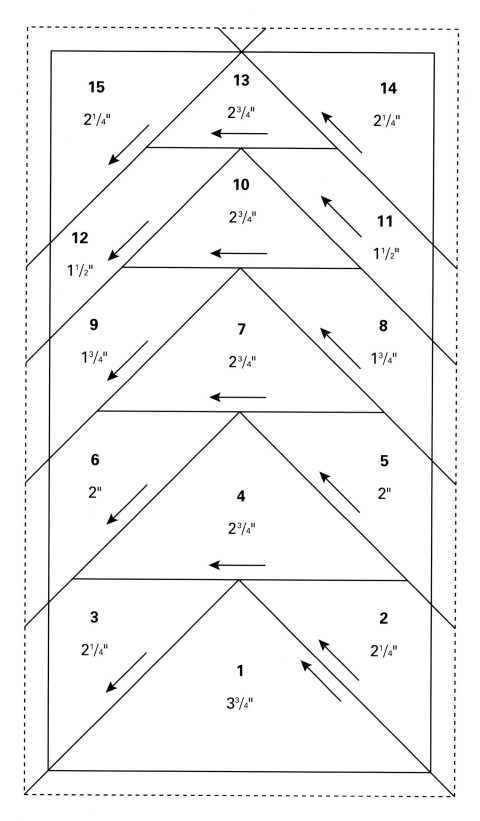

Shrinking Flying Geese pattern B

Make 4 copies.

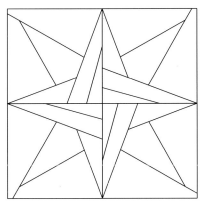

When designing your own
quilt, copy and color this
sample block as you wish.

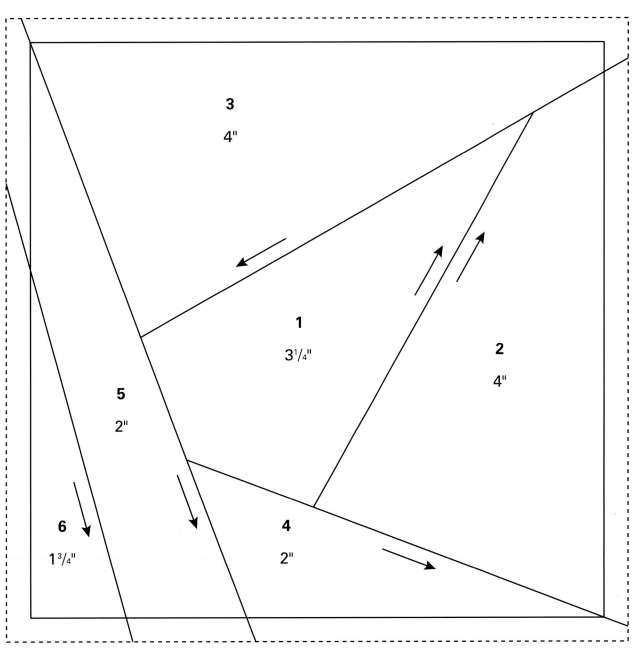

3

4"

1

$3\frac{1}{4}$"

2

4"

5

2"

6

$1\frac{3}{4}$"

4

2"

Simple Star pattern

Make 4 copies.

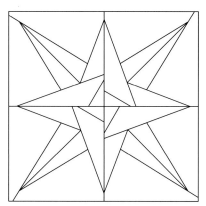

When designing your own quilt, copy and color this sample block as you wish.

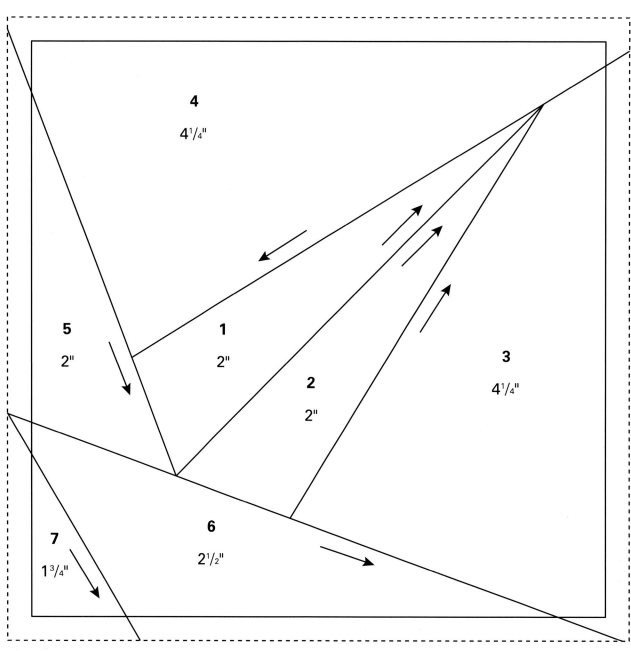

4

$4\frac{1}{4}$"

5

2"

1

2"

2

2"

3

$4\frac{1}{4}$"

6

$2\frac{1}{2}$"

7

$1\frac{3}{4}$"

Stargaze pattern

Make 4 copies.

When designing your own quilt, copy and color this sample block as you wish.

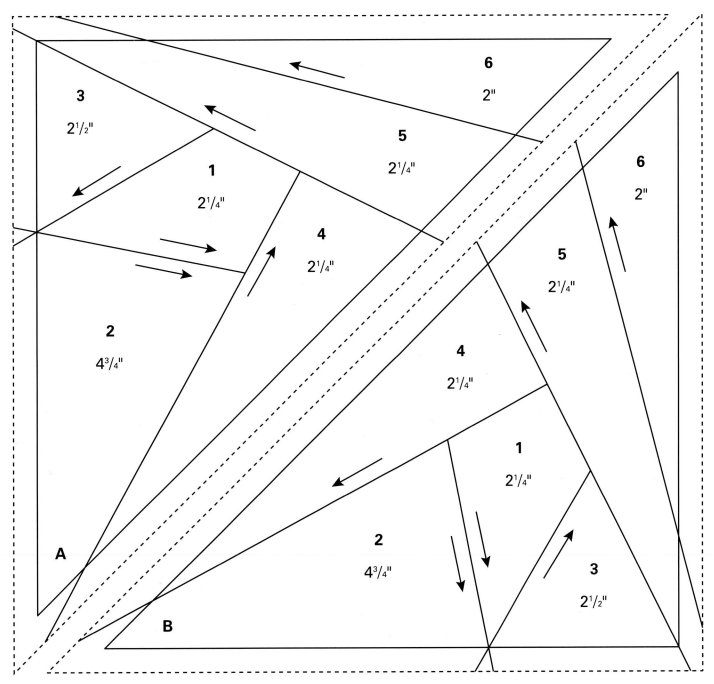

3

$2^1/_2$"

6

2"

1

$2^1/_4$"

5

$2^1/_4$"

4

$2^1/_4$"

6

2"

2

$4^3/_4$"

5

$2^1/_4$"

4

$2^1/_4$"

1

$2^1/_4$"

A

2

$4^3/_4$"

3

$2^1/_2$"

B

Faceted Star patterns A and B ~ Make 4 copies of each.

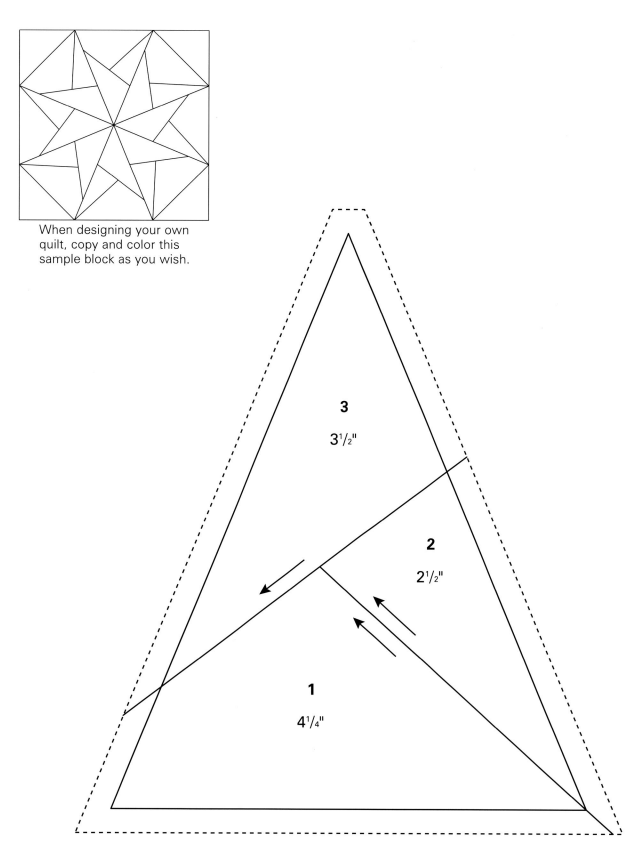

When designing your own
quilt, copy and color this
sample block as you wish.

3

3¹/₂"

2

2¹/₂"

1

4¹/₄"

Uneven Star pattern

Make 8 copies.

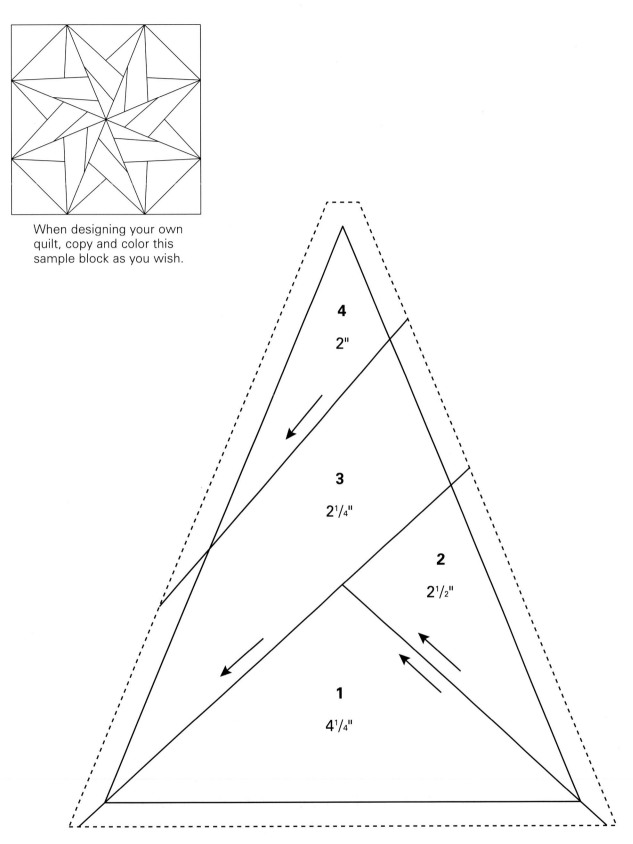

When designing your own quilt, copy and color this sample block as you wish.

4

2"

3

2¹/₄"

2

2¹/₂"

1

4¹/₄"

Twisted Star pattern

Make 8 copies.

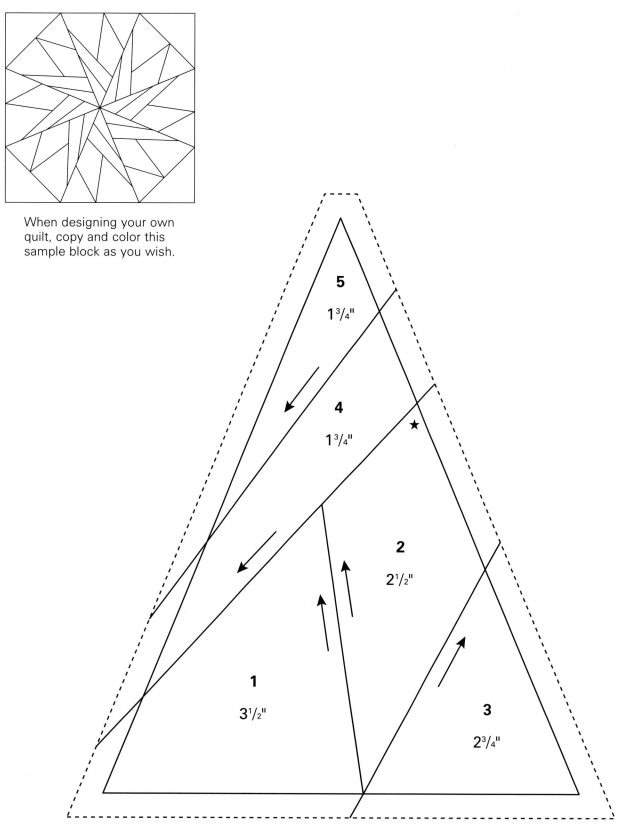

When designing your own quilt, copy and color this sample block as you wish.

5

$1^3/_4$"

4

$1^3/_4$"

★

2

$2^1/_2$"

1

$3^1/_2$"

3

$2^3/_4$"

Whirling Star pattern

Make 8 copies.

★ Be sure to allow enough fabric on strip to cover this point when piecing and trimming.

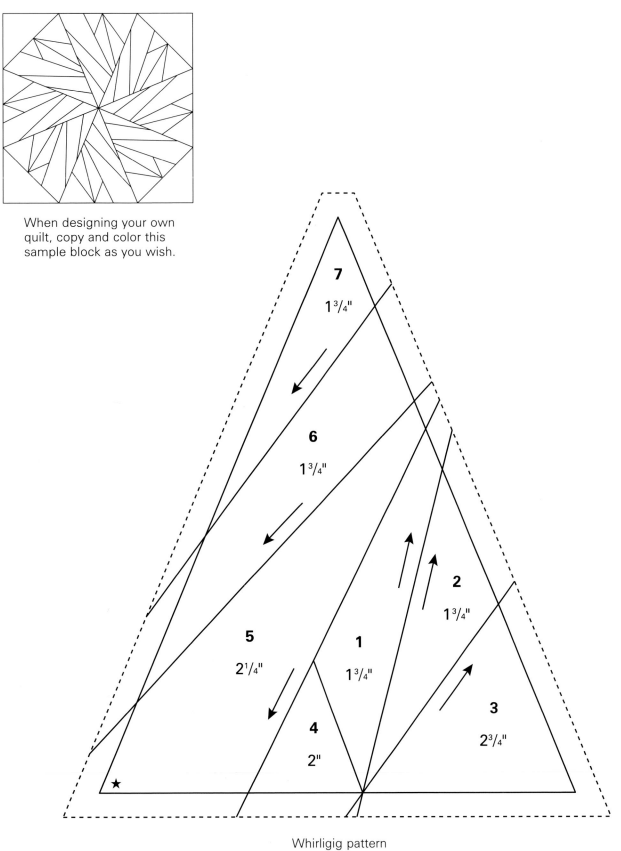

When designing your own quilt, copy and color this sample block as you wish.

7
$1^3/_4$"

6
$1^3/_4$"

2
$1^3/_4$"

5
$2^1/_4$"

1
$1^3/_4$"

3
$2^3/_4$"

4
2"

Whirligig pattern

Make 8 copies.

★ Be sure to allow enough fabric on strip to cover this point when piecing and trimming.

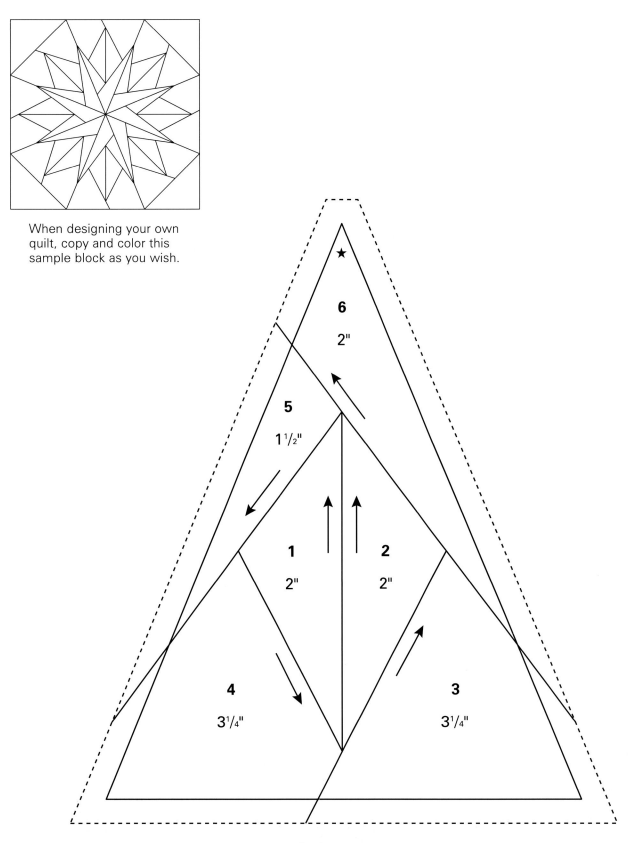

When designing your own quilt, copy and color this sample block as you wish.

6

2"

5

1¹/₂"

1

2"

2

2"

4

3¹/₄"

3

3¹/₄"

Starburst pattern

Make 8 copies.

★ Be sure to allow enough fabric on strip to cover this point when piecing and trimming.

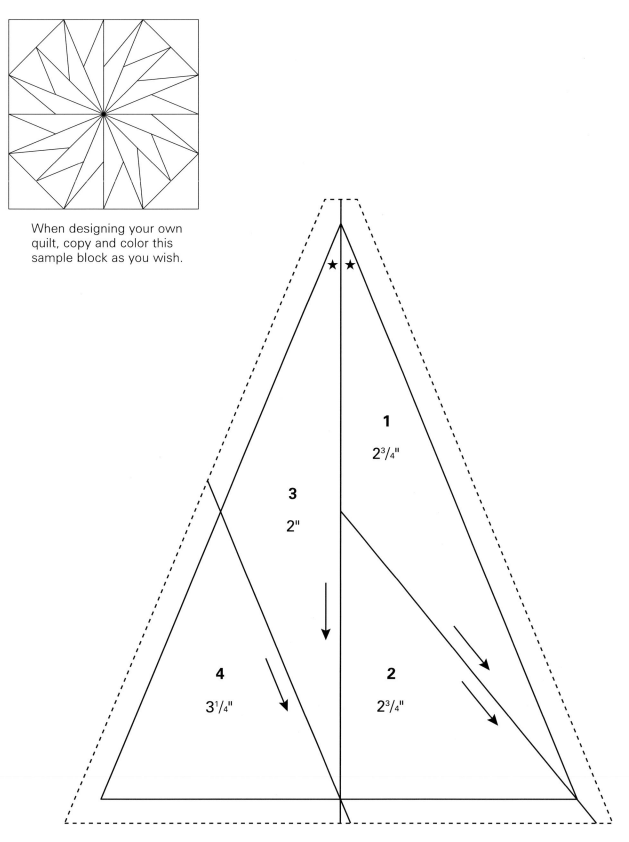

When designing your own quilt, copy and color this sample block as you wish.

1

$2^3/_4"$

3

$2"$

4

$3^1/_4"$

2

$2^3/_4"$

Radiant Star pattern

Make 8 copies.

★ Be sure to allow enough fabric on strip to cover these points when piecing and trimming.

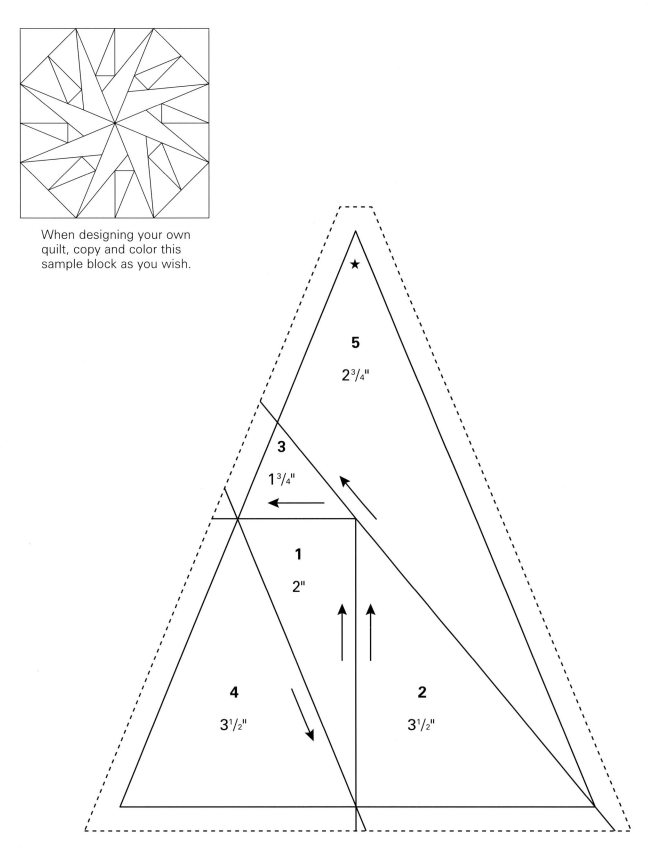

When designing your own quilt, copy and color this sample block as you wish.

5

$2^3/_4$"

3

$1^3/_4$"

1

2"

4

$3^1/_2$"

2

$3^1/_2$"

Cattywampus Star pattern

Make 8 copies.

★ Be sure to allow enough fabric on strip to cover this point when piecing and trimming.

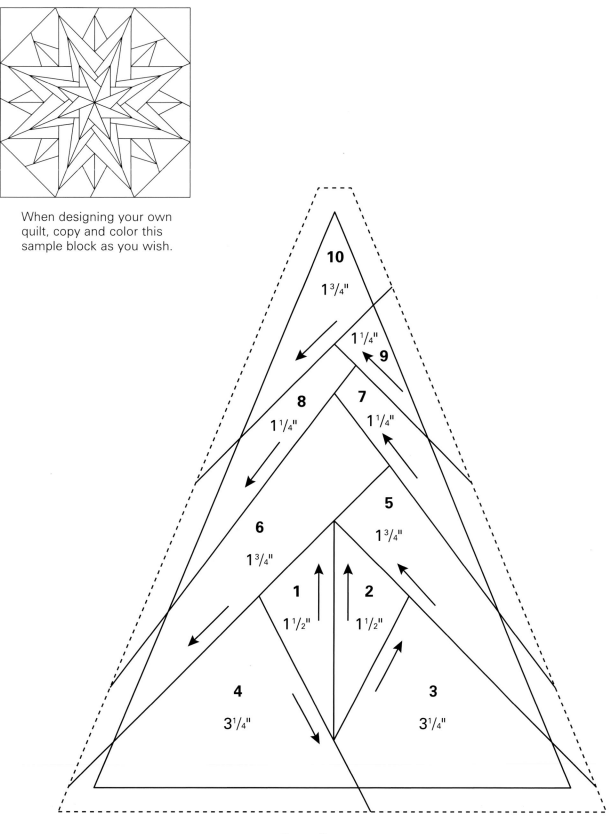

When designing your own quilt, copy and color this sample block as you wish.

10

$1^3/4"$

$1^1/4"$ **9**

8 **7**

$1^1/4"$ $1^1/4"$

5

6 $1^3/4"$

$1^3/4"$

1 **2**

$1^1/2"$ $1^1/2"$

4 **3**

$3^1/4"$ $3^1/4"$

Super Star pattern

Make 8 copies.

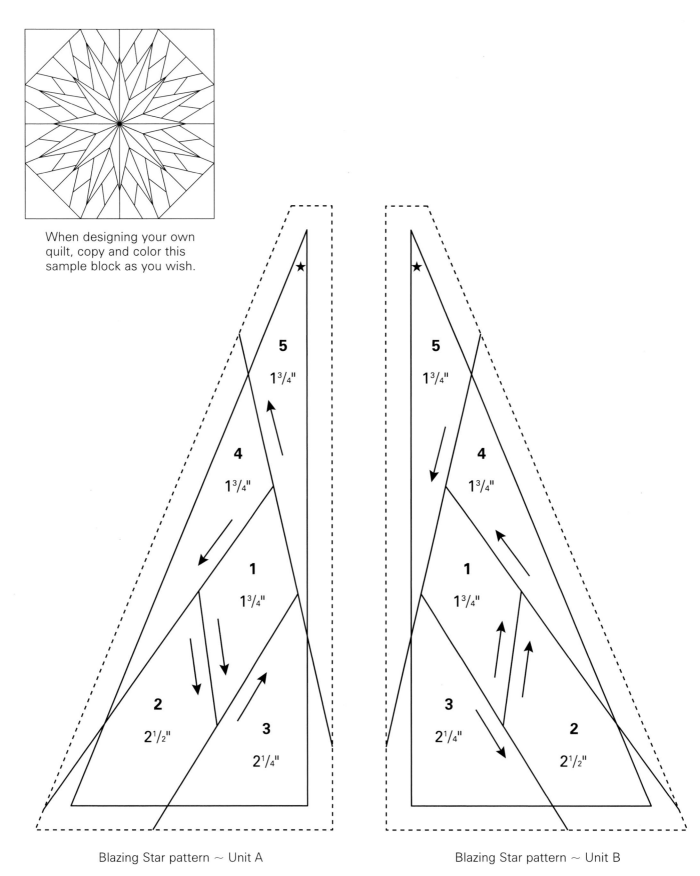

When designing your own
quilt, copy and color this
sample block as you wish.

5

$1^3/_4$"

4

$1^3/_4$"

1

$1^3/_4$"

2

$2^1/_2$"

3

$2^1/_4$"

5

$1^3/_4$"

4

$1^3/_4$"

1

$1^3/_4$"

3

$2^1/_4$"

2

$2^1/_2$"

Blazing Star pattern ~ Unit A

Blazing Star pattern ~ Unit B

Make 8 copies of each.

★ Be sure to allow enough fabric on strip to cover these points when piecing and trimming.

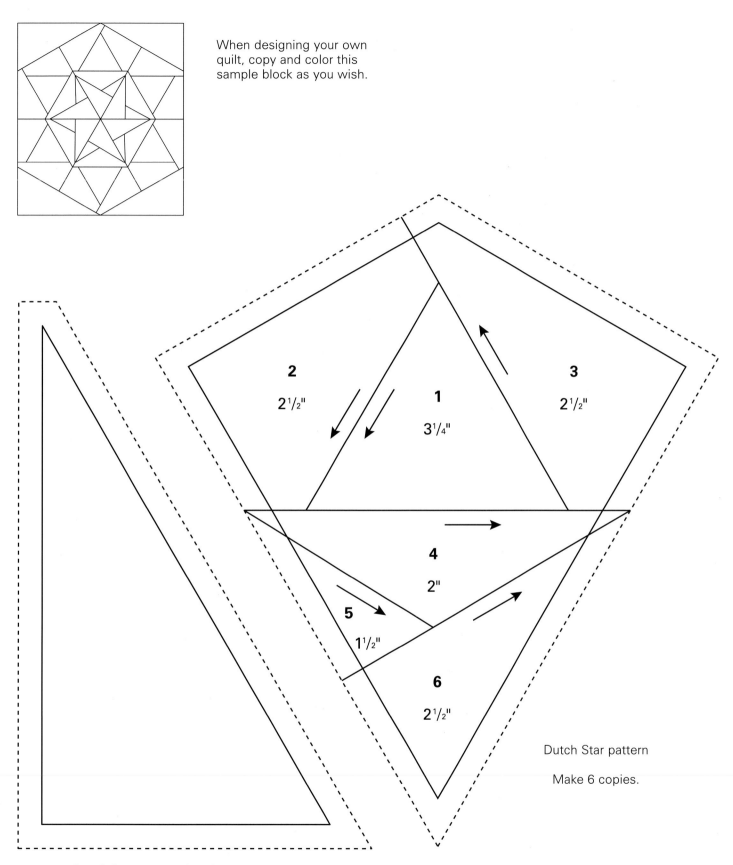

When designing your own quilt, copy and color this sample block as you wish.

2

$2^{1}/_{2}$"

1

$3^{1}/_{4}$"

3

$2^{1}/_{2}$"

4

2"

5

$1^{1}/_{2}$"

6

$2^{1}/_{2}$"

Dutch Star pattern

Make 6 copies.

Dutch Star corner triangle pattern

Cut 2 as shown and 2 reversed.

Gallery of Quilts

This collection includes quilts that my students and I have made using the Quick-Strip Paper-Piecing technique. I designed a group of block patterns and presented them to my students in a workshop. Each person then chose a block or blocks to work with and designed her own unique quilt.

inspiring

Quilt size: 58¹/₂" x 58¹/₂"

RASPBERRY RIPPLE

Made by Peggy Martin, 2002
Quilted by Laurie Daniells

The Simple Star and Whirling Star are alternated with Serendipity
blocks. A Serendipity border completes the pattern around
the blocks.

Quilt size: 51" x 51"

A PAIR OF STRANGERS

Made and quilted by Mary Tabar, 2002

An arrangement of Serendipity blocks in bold colors is set on point
and bordered with an original setting. Mary added triangles of
shiny metallic fabrics to give the quilt sparkle.

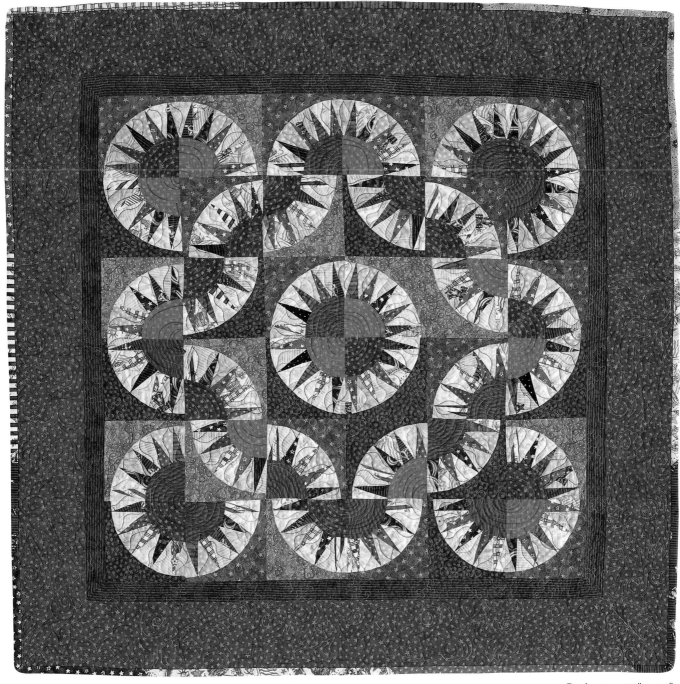

Quilt size: 48" x 48"

AMERICAN BEAUTY

Made by Nancy Amidon, 2002
Quilted by Jubilee Quilted Creations

This is a truly scrappy version of the New York Beauty done in
patriotic red, white, and blue fabrics in a barn-raising set.

Quilt size: 53¹/₂" x 66"

GARDEN OF STARS

Made and quilted by Karen Shell, 2002

Karen fell in love with all the great chintz fabrics that are
available and pieced these Simple Star blocks for a classic,
sophisticated look.

Quilt size: 63" x 52"

CELESTIAL CELEBRATION

Made by Jeanne Backman, 2002
Quilted by Cindy Feagle

Jeanne's masterful use of batiks is evident in this radiant quilt.

The *Stargaze* pattern is inventively set both straight and on point.

Quilt size: 50" x 50"

FACETED STAR

Made and quilted by Lois Russell, 2002

Lois used her scanner to reduce the Faceted Star pattern to about 8", then set the brightly colored blocks with three-quarter Faceted Star blocks in the corners as a unique border treatment.

Quilt size: 58" x 42"

BE CAREFUL WHAT YOU WISH FOR

Made by Sandra McCullough, 2002
Quilted by Linda Kamm

Uneven Star blocks pieced from glorious batik fabrics are set on
point on a rich purple background. Swirling quilting lines dance
across the surface.

Quilt size: 61½" x 92"

CRÈME DE MENTHE

Made by Lorraine Marstall, 2002
Quilted by Wendy Knight

Lorraine dedicated this quilt to her father, with fond memories
of many a "Grasshopper" and just once a "Pink Squirrel." She
designed the sashing for her Starburst pattern blocks and set it
with a pieced border.

Quilt size: 52" x 71½"

CELESTIAL CHECKERS

Made by Allegra Olson, 2002
Quilted by Faith

Super Star blocks are alternated with an original Checkerboard block. The border squares are a perfect complement to the quilt design.

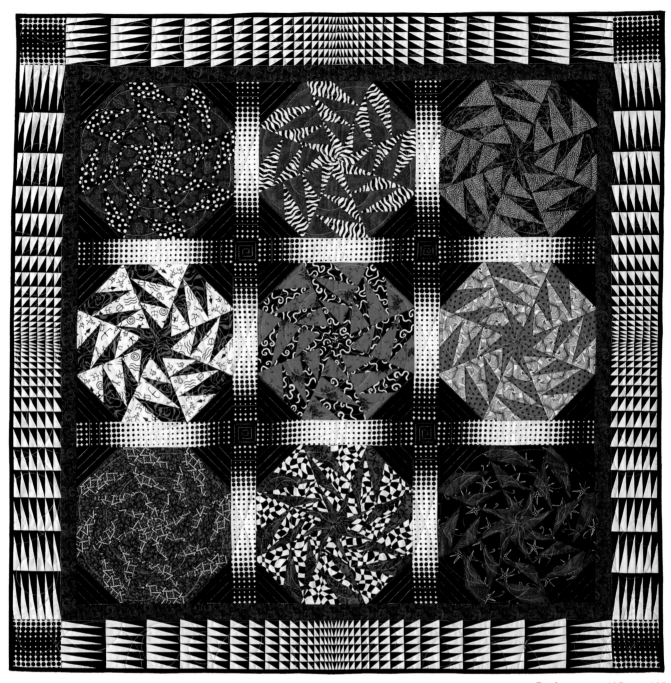

Quilt size: 48¹/₂" x 48¹/₂"

BRAMBLES AND ROSES

Made by Peggy Martin, 2002
Quilted by Wendy Knight

I love the graphic quality of red, black, and white together. The
black and white op-art fabrics in the sashing and borders seemed
to add the perfect finishing touch.

Quilt size: 44½" x 60½"

AT THE CIRCUS

Made and quilted by Peggy Martin, 2002

Spinning Star and Serendipity blocks mix well with traditionally
pieced blocks in this cheery strip-row sampler quilt.

I'M DREAMING OF A WHITE CHRISTMAS

Made and quilted by Kris Blundell-Mitchell, 2002

Paper-pieced snowflake blocks are set in Attic Windows. The
partial snowflake in the top window of the quilt gives a feeling of
anticipation and depth.

Quilt size: 42½" x 46"

SNOWFALL

Made and quilted by Peggy Martin, 2000

Paper-pieced snowflake blocks are set at angles, while other paper-cut snowflakes were sunprinted using fabric paints. The silver snowflakes were made with water-soluble stabilizer and metallic yarns in the bobbin. Silver thread completes the quilting.

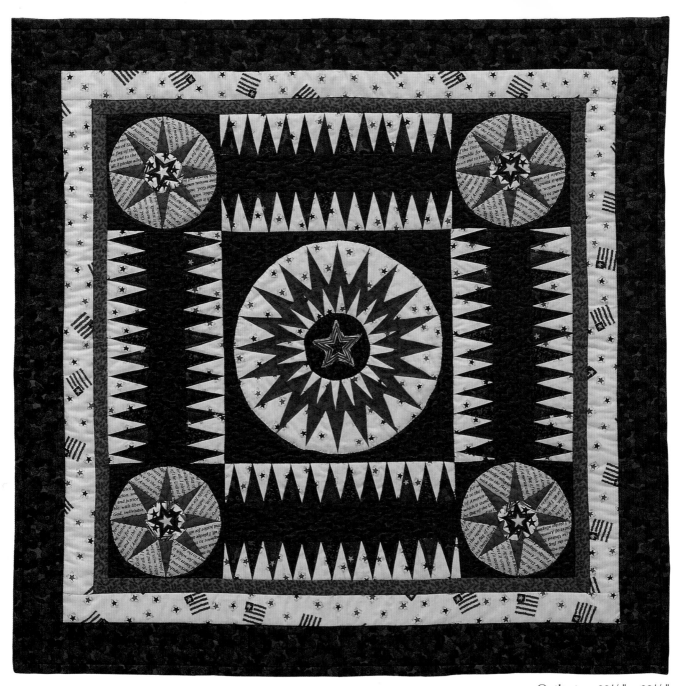

Quilt size: 32$\frac{1}{2}$" x 32$\frac{1}{2}$"

PATRIOTIC SUNFLOWER

Made and quilted by Allegra Olson, 2002

The traditional Sunflower block and borders are a breeze to piece using the Quick-Strip Paper-Piecing technique. Star, flag, and Pledge of Allegiance fabrics add to the patriotic theme.

Quilt size: 28" x 28"

SUPERNOVA

Made and quilted by Patricia Wolfe, 2002

The bright fabrics create a dramatic effect with the black print
background in this circle design.

Quilt size: 52½" x 52½"

COSMIC ENCOUNTERS

Made by Peggy Martin, 2002
Quilted by Laurie Daniells

Different circle designs, inspired by traditional Mariner's Compass
and Sunflower blocks, float on a lavender and peach sky. The
circles were pieced using the Quick-Strip Paper-Piecing method,
then appliquéd to the background.

General Instructions

Finishing your quilt is not always the most exciting part of quilting, but these finishing steps are very important. Good basting, quilting, and binding will not only help your quilts lie flat and look more beautiful, but will also help them stand the test of time.

Illuminating

General Instructions

Layering and Basting

1 Piece the back of your quilt as needed to make the backing 2"–3" larger than the quilt top on all sides. The batting should be the same size as the backing. Press the backing well so there are no wrinkles. Any seam allowances should be pressed to one side.

2 Layer the quilt and quilt top by laying the pressed backing on the bottom with the right side down, taped to the floor or a table. Then lay the batting in the middle and the pressed quilt top right side up on the top. Make sure that the backing and batting are flat with no wrinkles and that each layer is centered.

3 Baste from the center out using 1" safety pins if you are machine quilting, or a long needle (such as a long darner) and thread if you are hand quilting. Baste in a grid about 4"– 6" apart, always from the center outward.

Quilting

Hand or machine quilt as desired, stitching-in-the-ditch, or adding curves, contrary lines, or whatever strikes your fancy. Look at the photographs of how the quilts in this book were quilted, or look at the many good machine quilting books, stencils, and patterns that are available. Check your local quilt shop or online sources for ideas.

Binding

1 After you complete the quilting, trim all layers, squaring up corners and making sure all border edges are straight. Sometimes borders and corners will distort during the quilting process, and squaring them up ensures that your quilt will be square and flat.

2 Cut 2"-wide binding strips from selvage to selvage. It is not necessary to cut bias binding unless you want a plaid or stripe on the bias for a special effect. Cut enough strips to go around your quilt, plus at least 15" extra for mitering corners and meeting the ends.

3 Join binding strips to make a continuous binding by sewing a diagonal seam to prevent bulk. Put 2 strips right sides together, at a right angle. Sew at a diagonal and trim the seam to $1/4$". Press the seam open.

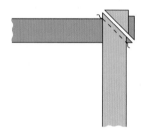

4 Fold binding strips in half lengthwise with the wrong sides together, and press so the binding is folded in a double layer.

5 Beginning near the middle of 1 side of your quilt and leaving a loose tail of 8"–10", sew the binding to the quilt top, match the raw edges and sew to $1/4$" from the corner, using a $1/4$" seam allowance. Stop and backstitch. Remove the quilt from the machine and clip threads.

6 To miter the corner, fold the free end of the binding up at a 90° angle so the raw edge of the binding lines up with the raw edge of the quilt.

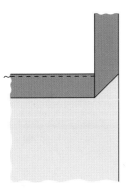

7 Fold the strip down on top of itself, so the raw edges line up with the raw edges on the right side of the quilt. The fold at the top will line up with the top edge of the quilt.

8 Begin sewing at the top folded edge of the binding, and sew down the side, using a ¹/₄" seam as before. Sew to ¹/₄" from the next corner, then repeat the mitering process as described above. Sew around the quilt until you are about 12" from where you began stitching. You will have a tail of binding left.

9 Select a point on the edge of the quilt top about midway between the two binding tails and mark with a pin or pencil mark.

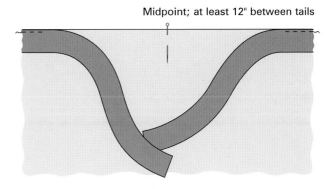

Midpoint; at least 12" between tails

10 Lay the left binding tail over the quilt top and mark only the top layer of binding with a pin at the previously marked midpoint. Move the left tail out of the way and measure the right binding tail in the same manner, laying the tail on the quilt and marking only the top layer of the binding with a pin at the previously marked midpoint.

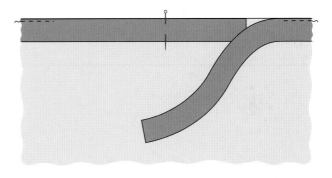

Lay left tail over midway point and mark top layer only.

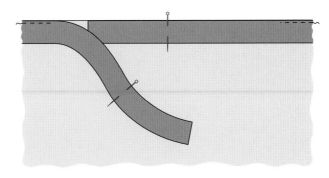

Lay right tail over midway point and mark top layer only.

11 Open up the left tail of the binding so it is right side up. Open up the right tail of the binding so it is right side down, and bring it to the left tail, matching the pin marks, and positioning the binding tails at right angles. Pin the strips together in this position to keep them at right angles. They will form an "X".

12 Where the pins or marks meet on the left side of the "X" is where you will begin sewing the seam to join the 2 tails. Sew across the junction of the "X".

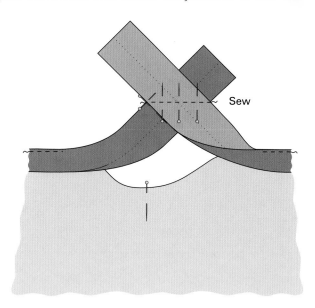

13 Fold the binding closed and check the fit with the quilt top. You will see the two long tails sticking up like long rabbit ears from the inside of the folded binding.

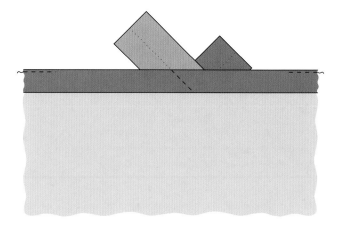

14 If the binding fits the quilt, trim the seam to ¹/₄″, and finger-press open or very carefully press with an iron. If you stretch the bias seam at this point it will no longer fit the edge of your quilt.

15 Fold the strip with wrong sides together again, making sure the diagonal seam stays open. Finish sewing the strip to the quilt, stitching over the previous stitches, and backstitching to lock stitching. The binding should fit your quilt and be no more bulky than any other joining seam.

16 Bring the folded edge of the binding to the back of the quilt and hand stitch in place on the back, folding in the miters at the corners. Make a label for your quilt with your name, the name of the quilt, and the date you completed it.

About the Author

Peggy Martin is an enthusiastic quilter and teacher who specializes in fast and accurate methods that offer many design possibilities. Colorplay and building variations on traditional quilts are her specialties. Her classes overflow with students eager to expand on tradition with their own creativity in color and design.

Learning to sew at the age of eight, she made most of her own clothes throughout her school, college, and early working years. She was introduced to quilting in 1981 and began teaching quilting classes in 1985. In Quick-Strip Paper Piecing, her first quilting book, she presents the innovative paper-piecing technique that she has been sharing with her students for years.

Peggy received a college degree in music, and when she is not busy quilting or teaching, she is playing her guitar or harp and singing folk music. She lives in San Diego and is married with two grown sons.

Resources

Here are a few of my favorite books that will provide you with more information about various aspects of quiltmaking. I've divided them into categories to make it a little easier to find what you're looking for.

Basic Quiltmaking

Hargrave, Harriet and Craig, Sharyn
The Art of Classic Quiltmaking
Lafayette, CA: C&T Publishing, 2000

From the Editors and Contributors of *Quilter's Newsletter Magazine* and *Quiltmaker* Magazine
All About Quilting from A to Z
Lafayette, CA: C&T Publishing, 2002

Color

Barnes, Christine
Color: The Quilter's Guide
Bothell, WA: That Patchwork Place, Inc., 1997

Wolfrom, Joen
Colorplay
Lafayette, CA: C&T Publishing, 2000

Paper Piecing:

Doak, Carol
40 Bright & Bold Paper-Pieced Blocks
Woodinville, WA: Martingale & Company, 2002

Garber, Gail
Stellar Journeys
Paducah, KY: American Quilter's Society, 2001

Wells, Valori
Radiant New York Beauties
Lafayette, CA: C&T Publishing, 2003

Index

Other Fine Books from C&T Publishing

For more information, write for a free catalog:
C&T Publishing, Inc.
P.O. Box 1456 • Lafayette, CA 94549
(800) 284-1114
Email: ctinfo@ctpub.com • Website: www.ctpub.com

For quilting supplies:
Cotton Patch Mail Order
3405 Hall Lane, Dept.CTB • Lafayette, CA 94549
(800) 835-4418 • (925) 283-7883
Email: quiltusa@yahoo.com • Website: www.quiltusa.com

Note: Fabrics used in the quilts shown may not be currently available since fabric manufacturers keep most fabrics in print for only a short time.